HBR Guide to
Smarter
Networking

Harvard Business Review Guides

Arm yourself with the advice you need to succeed on the job, from the most trusted brand in business. Packed with how-to essentials from leading experts, the HBR Guides provide smart answers to your most pressing work challenges.

The titles include:

HBR Guide for Women at Work

HBR Guide to Being a Great Boss

HBR Guide to Being More Productive

HBR Guide to Better Business Writing

HBR Guide to Better Mental Health at Work

HBR Guide to Building Your Business Case

HBR Guide to Buying a Small Business

HBR Guide to Changing Your Career

HBR Guide to Coaching Employees

HBR Guide to Collaborative Teams

HBR Guide to Crafting Your Purpose

HBR Guide to Data Analytics Basics for Managers

HBR Guide to Dealing with Conflict

HBR Guide to Delivering Effective Feedback

HBR Guide to Emotional Intelligence

HBR Guide to Finance Basics for Managers

HBR Guide to Flexible Work

HBR Guide to Getting the Mentoring You Need

HBR Guide to Getting the Right Job

HBR Guide to
Smarter
Networking

HARVARD BUSINESS REVIEW PRESS

Boston, Massachusetts

HBR Press Quantity Sales Discounts

Harvard Business Review Press titles are available at significant quantity discounts when purchased in bulk for client gifts, sales promotions, and premiums. Special editions, including books with corporate logos, customized covers, and letters from the company or CEO printed in the front matter, as well as excerpts of existing books, can also be created in large quantities for special needs.

For details and discount information for both print and ebook formats, contact booksales@harvardbusiness.org, tel. 800-988-0886, or www.hbr.org/bulksales.

The web addresses referenced in this book were live and correct at the time of the book's publication but may be subject to change.

Library of Congress Cataloging-in-Publication data is forthcoming.

ISBN: 978-1-64782-335-1
eISBN: 978-1-64782-336-8

The paper used in this publication meets the requirements of the American National Standard for Permanence of Paper for Publications and Documents in Libraries and Archives Z39.48-1992.

What You'll Learn

You know that you need to be doing a better job networking, but something always seems to get in the way. Perhaps you can't find the time to stay in touch with past colleagues amid so many urgent, competing needs in your work life. Maybe you think you can get away without reaching out to new contacts until you're getting ready for a job search. Or there's a chance you find networking unpleasant, inauthentic, and exhausting and just can't bring yourself to do it as much as you know you should.

But no matter what has been keeping you from being a better networker, there's hope. Too many of us have been thinking about networking in the wrong ways. It isn't just something that happens at conferences and events, and it isn't about making as many connections as we can—it's about strengthening the connections we have and putting ourselves in the right position to build new relationships. We need to be smart networkers every day because every day we need the support of our networks to do our jobs effectively, gain access to resources for ourselves and our teams, and advance.

This guide provides practical tips and approaches to help you build a diverse, supportive, and effective network, whether you're hoping to do your current job better, move up in your organization, find a great new role, or achieve your long-term career goals.

You'll learn how to:

- Develop a growth mindset around networking

- Ask questions that advance conversations beyond small talk

- Build connections at conferences that last longer than the weekend

- Find islands in a sea of strangers

- Host a gathering to bring together interesting and inspiring people

- Secure a spot on recruiters' radars—and stay there

- Accelerate your job search by getting back in touch

- Network more comfortably, even if you're an introvert

- Build a network with multiple layers of diversity

- Tell your career story through your online presence

- Reach out confidently and graciously to someone you've never met

- Overcome identity-related obstacles to networking

- Prevent reaching out from burning you out

- Keep your network healthy over the long haul

Contents

Contents

SECTION TWO

Great First Impressions

SECTION THREE

Connecting at Conferences and Events

SECTION FOUR

Networking to Land a Great Job

SECTION FIVE

Networking to Do Your Job Better

Contents

SECTION SIX

Remote, Virtual, and Social Media Networking

SECTION SEVEN

Overcoming Distinct Networking Challenges

Contents

Introduction: Building a Smarter Network

Take a moment and think about the word *network*. If you've read a business article, listened to a podcast, or watched a TED talk any time over the past decade, you know that high-quality, diverse professional networks lead to better job prospects and business opportunities. They expose us to new information, allow us to advance more quickly in our careers, and even help put innovative ideas into practice faster. And all this applies to new leaders, entry-level professionals, job seekers, entrepreneurs, in a word, everyone. If you want to reach your career goals, you need a great network.

Now take another moment and think about the word *networking*. Does it have the same positive associations? Is it something you look forward to or something that you put off and dread? For many, it's dread. If you fall into that category, networking reeks of being inauthentic and manipulative—research shows that even just *thinking* about it makes some people feel unclean. Or you may feel like it's unpleasant and seedy, evoking events that reek of social awkwardness, bad coffee, and desperate job seekers. Or that it conjures the forced fun of a boozy after-work party when what you really need to do is be at your desk making progress toward a deadline or in your kitchen getting dinner on the table for your family. Networks are more important to the way we work than ever—but networking feels stuck in the 1980s. It's no wonder that for so many of us improving and expanding our networks—and even staying in touch with old colleagues—is a New Year's resolution or quarterly goal that we put off again and again.

It's time to leave these stale and negative associations behind. Let's reconnect the process of networking to the goal you're trying to achieve: a strong professional community that will lift you up—and help you lift others up—throughout your career. Let's think beyond "working our connections" and think instead about building a truly diverse network based on learning and mutual support. When you forge relationships with people who are at different stages of their careers, with those who have skills you don't have, with those who come from different backgrounds from you, or who bring perspectives from outside your industry—these are the people who will challenge you and encourage you to think differently, the ones who will push you to grow and move forward. No matter where you are on your journey, the *HBR Guide to Smarter Networking* will help you create and sustain these relationships.

The tips and advice in this book come from a wide range of HBR experts, and they approach the topic from every angle. Their findings are backed by research—but that doesn't mean there's a single right way to network. As you look through the table of contents, feel free to skip ahead to the chapters that sound the most relevant to you and put them into practice immediately. Or if you prefer to get the whole picture before leaping in, you can read in sequence.

If you want a deeper understanding of why your network matters to your career, start with section 1, "Why You Need to Network, Even If You're Not Job Hunting." You'll learn how the higher you rise at work, the more important your connections are to your job performance, and how different aspects of your network will support your operational, developmental, and strategic goals. And if you're among the many who don't feel excited about networking, be sure to read chapter 2, "Learn to Love Networking."

Your goal in developing your network should be to grow deep connections with the right people, not to exchange contact information with as many as possible. Section 2, "Great First Impressions," will help you have authentic initial conversations that go beyond small talk and help your new connections understand who you are and where you're going, not just what you do at work and what you want from them.

Conferences and networking events may not be your favorite activity—but you can still find ways to get more out of them whether you attend in person or virtually. Section 3, "Connecting at Conferences and Events," will encourage you to "pre-introduce" yourself before the conference begins, take on a more prominent role as a member of a panel, and manage your energy with intention. Or you might choose to sit out public events entirely and organize a smaller gathering of your own.

Browsing job sites is no longer sufficient for finding the best positions. Section 4, "Networking to Land a Great Job," explores how to tap into the vast ocean of underpublicized jobs. This can mean cultivating new connections through informational interviews, finding effective ways to get onto recruiters' radars, and making serendipity work for you by reaching out methodically to your extended network.

Section 5, "Networking to Do Your Job Better," reminds us that we can't take a break from developing our networks just because we're not planning on searching for a job anytime soon. Whether you're new in your role or well established, a network that is diverse in multiple dimensions—one that includes people who are very different from you and those who work outside your industry—will strengthen your ability to generate creative ideas, persuade others, and access sponsors who will create opportunities for you.

More and more outreach, initial introductions, and first meetings are happening over screens. While this can mean greater access to a wider range of individuals worldwide, it can also make it harder to break through amid all of the online noise. Section 6, "Remote, Virtual, and Social Media Networking," will help you stand out and get the right kind of attention instead of being scrolled past or deleted. This means creating online profiles that tell stories about you and your career, rather than listing your accomplishments in bullet points and learning how to write messages that start conversations rather than ask for favors.

It's undeniable that networking means navigating power dynamics—and understanding that sometimes these situations will be inequitable. Your gender, race, nationality, economic background, or family status may work against you as you seek to build an effective network. Even so, different approaches to networking can mitigate some of these structural disadvantages, and in certain situations, some identity-based traits can actually help you reach your networking goals. In section 7, "Overcoming Distinct Networking Challenges," we'll look at some of these difficult scenarios along with the opportunities they present.

Everyone has their own threshold for how much networking is too much. Section 8, "Avoiding Networking Burnout," focuses on acknowledging and respecting those limits, especially if you are the kind of person who needs to recharge after socializing. Sometimes that means slowing down, choosing quality over quantity, taking a break during an event, or politely declining the next networking opportunity.

Building a strong network is a long-term goal, and it doesn't always follow a clear path. The network you need today might not be the same one you need tomorrow or 10 years from now. Sometimes you'll let a friendship grow dormant when you shouldn't, or you'll find that you're putting a lot of effort into a relationship that's unreciprocated. You may realize that you're devoting too much time to making new contacts rather than keeping in touch with those who have always come through for you in the past. Section 9, "Sustaining Your Network over the Years," helps you take an intentional approach to keeping up and nurturing relationships over the long haul.

As you learn these new skills and approaches, try out the ones that feel the most natural and comfortable to you *and* that are the most beneficial to your career. Give one a shot the next time you introduce yourself. Talk about your goals for an upcoming conference with your colleagues ahead of time. Find 30 minutes a week to help someone in your network. If your first attempt with one of these new methods doesn't feel right, think about how you might tweak it for the next time or give another one a try. Even better, talk about what you attempted *with* someone in your network and workshop a better technique together. Above all, focus on what you'll learn, approach your networking conversations with curiosity, and treat them as an opportunity for discovery. Turn the page to take the first steps toward building the network that will help you succeed today and support you throughout the rest of your career.

Why You Need to Network, Even If You're Not Job Hunting

CHAPTER 1

A Smarter Way to Network

by Rob Cross and Robert J. Thomas

One of the happiest, most successful executives we know is a woman named Deb. She works at a major technology company and runs a global business unit that has more than 7,000 employees. When you ask her how she rose to the top and why she enjoys her job, her answer is simple: people. She points to her boss, the CEO, a mentor who "always has her back"; Steve, the head of a complementary business, with whom she has monthly brainstorming lunches and occasional gripe sessions; and Tom, a protégé to whom she has delegated responsibility for a large portion of her division. Outside the company,

---

Adapted from an article in *Harvard Business Review*, July–August 2011 (product #R1107P).

Deb's circle includes her counterparts in three strategic partnerships, who inspire her with new ideas; Sheila, a former colleague, now in a different industry, who gives her candid feedback; and her husband, Bob, an executive at a philanthropic organization. She also has close relationships with her fellow volunteers in a program for at-risk high school students and the members of her tennis group and book club.

This is Deb's social network (the real-world kind, not the virtual kind), and it has helped her career a lot. But not because the group is large or full of high-powered contacts. Her network is effective because it both supports and challenges her. Deb's relationships help her gain influence, broaden her expertise, learn new skills, and find purpose and balance. Deb values and nurtures them. "Make friends so that you have friends when you need friends" is her motto.

"My current role is really a product of a relationship I formed over a decade ago that came back to me at the right time," she explains. "People may chalk it up to luck, but I think more often than not luck happens through networks where people give first and are authentic in all they do."

Over the past 15 years, we've worked with many executives like Deb, at more than 300 companies. What began as organizational research—helping management teams understand and capitalize on the formal and informal social networks of their employees—has since metamorphosed into personal programs, which teach individual executives to increase their effectiveness by leveraging their networks.

The old adage "It's not what you know, it's who you know" is true. But it's more nuanced than that. In spite of what most self-help books say, network size doesn't usually matter. In fact, we've found that individuals who simply know a lot of people are less likely to achieve standout performance, because they're spread too thin. Political animals with lots of connections to corporate and industry leaders don't win the day, either. Yes, it's important to know powerful people, but if they account for too much of your network, your peers and subordinates often perceive you to be overly self-interested, and you may lose support as a result.

The data we've collected point to a different model for networking. The executives who consistently rank in the top 20% of their companies in both performance and well-being have diverse but select networks like Deb's—made up of high-quality relationships with people who come from several different spheres and from up and down the corporate hierarchy. These high performers, we have found, tap into six critical kinds of connections, which enhance their careers and lives in a variety of ways.

Through our work advising individual managers, we've also identified a four-step process that will help any executive develop this kind of network. But first, let's take a look at some common networking mistakes.

Getting It Wrong

Many people take a misguided approach to networking. They go astray by building imbalanced networks, pursuing the wrong kind of relationships, or leveraging

THREE COMMON TRAPS

In our work, we have identified six common managerial types who get stuck in three kinds of network traps. Do any of the descriptions below fit you?

The Wrong Structure

The formalist focuses too heavily on his company's official hierarchy, missing out on the efficiencies and opportunities that come from informal connections.

The overloaded manager has so much contact with colleagues and external ties that she becomes a bottleneck to progress and burns herself out.

The Wrong Relationships

The disconnected expert sticks with people who keep him focused on safe, existing competencies, rather than those who push him to build new skills.

The biased leader relies on advisers much like herself (same functional background, location, or values), who reinforce her biases, when she should instead seek outsiders to prompt more fully informed decisions.

The Wrong Behavior

The superficial networker engages in surface-level interaction with as many people as possible, mistakenly believing that a bigger network is a better one.

The chameleon changes his interests, values, and personality to match those of whatever subgroup is his audience and winds up being disconnected from every group.

relationships ineffectively. (See the sidebar "Three Common Traps") These people might remain successful for a time, but often they will hit a plateau or see their career derailed because their networks couldn't prompt or support a critical transition.

Consider Dan, the chief information officer of one of the world's largest life sciences organizations. He was under constant pressure to find new technologies that would spur innovation and speed the drug commercialization process at his company, and he needed a network that would help him. Unfortunately, more than 70% of his trusted advisers were in the unit he had worked in before becoming CIO. Not only did they reinforce his bias toward certain solutions and vendors, but they lacked the outside knowledge he needed. "I had started to mistake friendship, trust, and accessibility for real expertise in new domains," he told us. "This didn't mean I was going to dump these people, as they played important roles for me in other ways. But I needed to be more targeted in who I let influence my thinking."

Another overarching mistake we often see in executives' networks is an imbalance between connections that promote career advancement and those that promote engagement and satisfaction. Numerous studies have shown that happier executives are higher-performing ones.

Take Tim, the director of a large practice area at a leading professional services firm. On the surface he was doing well, but job stress had taken its toll. He was 40 pounds overweight, with alarmingly high cholesterol and blood sugar levels, and prone to extreme mood swings. When things went well at work, he was happy; when they didn't, he wasn't pleasant to be around. In fact, Tim's wife finally broke down and told him she thought he had become a career-obsessed jerk and needed to get other interests. With her encouragement, he joined Habitat for Humanity and started rowing with their daughter. As a result, his social network expanded to include people with different perspectives and values, who helped him focus on more healthful and fulfilling pursuits. "As I spent more time with different groups, what I cared about diversified," he says. "Physically, I'm in much better shape and probably staved off a heart attack. But I think I'm a better leader, too, in that I think about problems more broadly, and I'm more resilient. Our peer feedback systems are also clearly indicating that people are more committed to the new me."

Getting It Right

To understand more about what makes an effective network, let's look again at Deb. She has a small set of core contacts—14 people she really relies on. Effective core networks typically range in size from 12 to 18 people. But what really matters is structure: Core connections must bridge smaller, more-diverse kinds of groups and cross hierarchical, organizational, functional, and geographic lines. Core relationships should result in more learning, less bias in decision-making, and greater personal growth and balance. The people in your inner circle should also model positive behaviors, because if those around you are enthusiastic, authentic, and generous, you will be, too.

More specifically, our data show that high performers have strong ties to:

1. people who offer them new information or expertise, including internal or external clients, who increase their market awareness; peers in other functions, divisions, or geographies, who share best practices; and contacts in other industries, who inspire innovation;

2. formally powerful people, who provide mentoring, sense-making, political support, and resources; and informally powerful people, who offer influence, help coordinating projects, and support among the rank and file; and

3. people who give them developmental feedback, challenge their decisions, and push them to be better. At an early career stage, an employee might get this from a boss or customers; later, it tends to come from coaches, trusted colleagues, or a spouse.

Meanwhile, the most satisfied executives have ties to:

1. people who provide personal support, such as colleagues who help them get back on track when they're having a bad day or friends with whom they can just be themselves;

2. people who add a sense of purpose or worth, such as bosses and customers who validate their work, and family members and other stakeholders who show them work has a broader meaning; and

3. people who promote their work-life balance, holding them accountable for activities that improve their physical health (such as sports), mental engagement (such as hobbies or educational classes), or spiritual well-being (music, religion, art, or volunteer work).

How does one create such a varied network? We recommend a four-point action plan: analyze, de-layer, diversify, and capitalize.

Analyze

Start by looking at the individuals in your network. Where are they located—are they within your team, your unit, or your company, or outside your organization? What benefits do your interactions with them provide? How energizing are those interactions?

The last question is an important one. Energizers bring out the best in everyone around them, and our data show that having them in your network is a strong predictor of success over time. These people aren't necessarily extroverted or charismatic. They're people who always see opportunities, even in challenging situations, and create room for others to meaningfully contribute. Good energizers are trustworthy and committed to principles larger than their self-interest, and they enjoy other people. "De-energizers," by contrast, are quick to point out obstacles, critique people rather than ideas, are inflexible in their thinking, fail to create opportunities, miss commitments, and don't show concern for others. Unfortunately, energy-sapping interactions have more impact than energizing ones—up to seven times as much, according to one study. And our own research suggests that roughly 90% of anxiety at work is created by 5% of one's network—the people who sap energy.

Next, classify your relationships by the benefits they provide. Generally, benefits fall into one of six basic categories: information, political support and influence, personal development, personal support and energy, a sense of purpose or worth, and work-life balance. It's important to have people who provide each kind of benefit in your network. Categorizing your relationships will give you a clearer idea of whether your network is extending your abilities or keeping you stuck. You'll see where you have holes and redundancies and which people you depend on too much—or not enough.

Let's use Joe, a rising star in an investment bank, as a case study. He had 24 close advisers—on the surface, a more than healthy number. But many of the people he relied on were from his own department and frequently relied on one another. If he eliminated those redundancies, his network shrank to five people. After giving it some thought and observing his peers' networks, he realized he was missing links with several important types of people: colleagues focused on financial offerings outside his own products, who could help him deliver broader financial solutions to customers; coworkers in different geographies—particularly London and Asia—who could enhance his ability to sell to global clients; and board-level relationships at key accounts, who could make client introductions and influence purchasing decisions. His insularity was limiting his options and hurting his chances of promotion to managing director. He realized he would need to focus on cultivating a network rather than allowing it to organically arise from the day-to-day demands of his work.

De-layer

Once you've analyzed your network, you need to make some hard decisions about which relationships to back away from. First, look at eliminating or minimizing contact with people who sap you of energy or promote unhealthful behaviors. You can do this by reshaping your role to avoid them, devoting less time to them, working to change their behavior, or reframing your reactions so that you don't dwell on the interactions.

John, an academic, realized that two university administrators in his network were causing him a great deal of anxiety. This had so soured his view of his school that he was considering leaving. He therefore decided to devote less time to projects and committees that would involve the negative contacts and to avoid dwelling on any sniping comments they subjected him to. Within a year he was much more productive and happy. "By shifting my role and how I reacted to the idiots, I turned a negative situation around," John says. "In hindsight it was an obvious move—rather than leave a place I loved—but emotions can spiral on you in ways you don't recognize."

The next step is to ask yourself which of the six categories have too many people in them. Early-stage leaders, for example, tend to focus too much on information and not enough on personal development and might want to shed some of the contacts who give them the former to make more time for those who give them the latter.

18

Beyond this, consider which individuals—and types of people as determined by function, hierarchy, or geography—have too much of you, and why. Is the cause structural, in that work procedures require you to be involved? Or is your own behavior causing the imbalance? What can you change to rectify the situation? Too often we see leaders fail because they accept or create too many collaborative demands.

Paul, the head of research in a consumer products company, had a network of almost 70 people just at work. But he got many complaints from people who said they needed greater access to him. His productivity, and his unit's, was suffering. When he analyzed his network, he realized that he was missing "people and initiatives one or two levels out." To address this, he decided to delegate—stepping away from interactions that didn't require his presence and cultivating "go to" stand-ins in certain areas of expertise. He also changed his leadership style from extraordinarily accessible to helpful but more removed, which encouraged subordinates to solve their own problems by connecting with people around him. "As a leader you can find yourself in this bubble of activity where you feel like a lot is happening moving from meeting to meeting," Paul says. "You can actually start to thrive on this in some ways. I had to move past this for us to be effective as a unit and so that I could be more forward-thinking."

Diversify

Now that you've created room in your network, you need to fill it with the right people. Simple tools like worksheets can help you get started. For example, you might make a list of the six categories of relationships and think about colleagues who could fill the holes you have in each. Remember to focus on positive, energetic, selfless people, and be sure to ask people inside and outside your network for recommendations.

You should also think about how you could connect your network to your professional and personal goals. Here's another simple exercise: Write down three specific business results you hope to achieve over the next year (such as doubling sales or winning an Asia-based client) and then list the people (by name or general role) who could help you with them, thanks to their expertise, control over resources, or ability to provide political support. Joe, the investment banker, identified counterparts in the Asian and European operations of his company who had relationships with the clients he was focused on and then scheduled regular calls with them to coordinate efforts. "In a couple of cases this helped me identify opportunities I could pitch proactively. In others it just helped us appear more coordinated when we were competing against other banks," he says. One of the big challenges for Paul, the consumer products executive, was managing a new facility and line of innovation in China. Because none of his trusted advisers had ever even been to that country, he reached out to the head of R&D at a major life-sciences organization that had undertaken a similar effort.

Capitalize

Last, make sure you're using your contacts as effectively as you can. Are there people you rely on in one sphere, such as political support, that you could also use to fill a need in another, such as personal development? Could you get more out of some relationships if you put more energy into them? Our research shows, for instance, that high performers at all levels tend to use their information contacts to gain other benefits, such as new ideas. Reciprocal relationships also tend to be more fruitful; the most successful leaders always look for ways to give more to their contacts.

Alan, a top executive at a global insurance company, realized that although he had a good network, he was still making decisions in relative isolation. He failed to elicit insights from others and, as a result, wasn't making enough progress toward his goals. So he started inviting his more-junior contacts, who were informal opinion leaders in his company, to lunch and asking them open-ended questions. These conversations led him to streamline decision-making and uncover innovation deep within the firm's hierarchy. "When I met with one lady, I was stunned at a great new product idea she had been pushing for months," Alan says. "But she hadn't been able to get the right people to listen. I was able to step in and help make things happen. To me the right way to be tapping into people is in this exploratory way—whether it is about strategic insights or just how they think I'm doing on some aspect of my job. That's how I get to new ways of thinking and doing things, and I know it makes me much more effective than people who are smarter than me."

A network constructed using this four-point model will build on itself over time. In due course, it will ensure that the best opportunities, ideas, and talent come your way.

————————

Rob Cross is the Edward A. Madden Professor of Global Leadership at Babson College, founder of the Connected Commons, and the author of *Beyond Collaboration Overload* (Harvard Business Review Press, 2021). **Robert J. Thomas** is a managing director of Accenture Strategy. He is the author of eight books on leadership and organizational change, including *Crucibles of Leadership, Geeks and Geezers* (with Warren Bennis), and *Driving Results through Social Networks* (with Rob Cross).

CHAPTER 2

Learn to Love Networking

by Francesca Gino, Maryam Kouchaki, and Tiziana Casciaro

"I hate networking." We hear this all the time from executives, other professionals, and MBA students. They tell us that networking makes them feel uncomfortable and phony—even dirty. Although some people have a natural passion for it—namely, the extroverts who love and thrive on social interaction—many understandably see it as brown-nosing, exploitative, and inauthentic.

But in today's world, networking is a necessity. A mountain of research shows that professional networks lead to more job and business opportunities, broader and

Adapted from an article in *Harvard Business Review*, May 2016 (product #R1605J).

deeper knowledge, improved capacity to innovate, faster advancement, and greater status and authority. Building and nurturing professional relationships also improves the quality of work and increases job satisfaction.

When we studied 165 lawyers at a large North American law firm, for example, we found that their success depended on their ability to network effectively both internally (to get themselves assigned to choice clients) and externally (to bring business into the firm). Those who regarded these activities as distasteful and avoided them had fewer billable hours than their peers.

Fortunately, our research shows that an aversion to networking can be overcome. We've identified four strategies to help people change their mindset.

1. Focus on Learning

Most people have a dominant motivational focus—what psychologists refer to as either a "promotion" or a "prevention" mindset. Those in the former category think primarily about the growth, advancement, and accomplishments that networking can bring them, while those in the latter see it as something they are obligated to take part in for professional reasons.

In laboratory experiments we conducted in the United States and Italy with college students and working adults, and in an additional sample of 174 lawyers at the firm we studied, we documented the effects of both types of thinking. Promotion-focused people networked because they wanted to and approached the activity with excitement, curiosity, and an open mind about all the possibilities that might unfold. Prevention-focused people saw networking as a necessary evil and felt inauthentic while engaged in it, so they did it less often and, as a result, underperformed in aspects of their jobs.

Thankfully, as Stanford University's Carol Dweck has documented in her research, it's possible to shift your mindset from prevention to promotion so that you see networking as an opportunity for discovery and learning rather than a chore.

Consider a work-related social function you feel obliged to attend. You can tell yourself, "I hate these kinds of events. I'm going to have to put on a show and schmooze and pretend to like it." Or you can tell yourself, "Who knows—it could be interesting. Sometimes when you least expect it, you have a conversation that brings up new ideas and leads to new experiences and opportunities."

If you are an introvert, you can't simply will yourself to be extroverted, of course. But everyone can choose which motivational focus to bring to networking. Concentrate on the positives—how it's going to help you boost the knowledge and skills that are needed in your job—and the activity will begin to seem much more worthwhile.

2. Identify Common Interests

The next step in making networking more palatable is to think about how your interests and goals align with those of people you meet and how that can help you forge meaningful working relationships. Northwestern University's Brian Uzzi calls this the shared activities principle. "Potent networks are not forged through casual interactions but through relatively high-stakes activities that connect you with diverse others," he explains. Numerous studies in social psychology have demonstrated that people establish the most collaborative and longest-lasting connections when they work together on tasks that require one another's contributions. Indeed, research that one of us (Tiziana) conducted with INSEAD's Miguel Sousa Lobo showed that this "task interdependence" can be one of the biggest sources of positive energy in professional relationships.

Consider the approach taken by Claude Grunitzky, a serial entrepreneur in the media industries, when he set out to meet Jefferson Hack, founder of the underground British style and music magazine *Dazed & Confused*. As described in the Harvard Business School case study "Claude Grunitzky," by Julie Battilana, Lakshmi Ramarajan, and James Weber, Grunitzky—then 22 and preparing to found his first business, an urban hip-hop magazine in London—learned everything he could about Hack.

"I read every one of his magazines, noticed what he was writing about and what kinds of bands he reviewed," Grunitzky recalled. "I did so much of this I felt I could almost understand his personality before we met." Armed with that knowledge and convinced that he and Hack had similar worldviews and aspirations, Grunitzky felt much more comfortable approaching the industry elder.

When your networking is driven by substantive, shared interests you've identified through serious research, it will feel more authentic and meaningful and is more likely to lead to relationships that have those qualities too.

3. Think Broadly About What You Can Give

Even when you do not share an interest with someone, you can probably find something valuable to offer by thinking beyond the obvious. Of course, this isn't always easy. We've found that people who feel powerless—because they are junior in their organizations, because they belong to an underrepresented group, or for other reasons—often believe they have too little to give and are therefore the least likely to engage in networking, even though they're the ones who will probably derive the most benefit from it.

This problem was highlighted in two studies we conducted at the law firm mentioned above, which involved different groups of lawyers at different points in time. We found that senior people were typically much more comfortable networking than junior people were because of their greater power in the organization. This makes sense. When people believe they have a lot to offer others, such as wise advice, mentorship, access, and resources, networking feels easier and less selfish.

A controlled experiment confirmed this finding: People in whom we induced feelings of power found networking less repulsive and were more willing to do it than people assigned to a condition that made them feel powerless.

However, even those with lower rank and less power almost certainly have more to offer than they realize. In their book *Influence Without Authority*, Allan Cohen and David Bradford note that most people tend to think too narrowly about the resources they have that others might value. They focus on tangible, task-related things such as money, social connections, technical support, and information, while ignoring less obvious assets such as gratitude, recognition, and enhanced reputation. For instance, although mentors typically like helping others, they tend to enjoy it all the more when they are thanked for their assistance.

The more heartfelt the expression of gratitude, the greater its value to the recipient. One young professional we know told us that when she turned 30, she wrote to the 30 people she felt had contributed the most to her professional growth, thanking them and describing the specific ways each had helped her. The recipients no doubt appreciated the personalized update and acknowledgment.

When gratitude is expressed publicly, it can also enhance an adviser's reputation in the workplace. Think of the effect you have when you sing your boss's praises to your colleagues and superiors, outlining all the ways you've progressed under his or her tutelage.

People also appreciate those who understand their values and identities and make them feel included. Juan, an Argentinian executive based in the Toronto office of a Canadian property management company, told us about Hendrik, a junior hire from Germany who rallied everyone in the office to join a series of soccer games that he single-handedly organized. His fellow expats—and there were many, because the company's workforce was internationally diverse—finally had something fun to do with their colleagues, and Hendrik's status and connections immediately shot up. In spite of his low-power position, he had brought something new to the table.

You might also have unique insights or knowledge that could be useful to those with whom you're networking. For example, junior people are often better informed than their senior colleagues about generational trends and new markets and technologies. Grunitzky is a prime example. "I knew I could bring something to [Jefferson Hack], which was expertise in hip-hop," he said. The relationship ended up being a two-way street.

When you think more about what you can give to others than what you can get from them, networking will seem less self-promotional and more selfless—and therefore more worthy of your time.

4. Find a Higher Purpose

Another factor that affects people's interest in and effectiveness at networking is the primary purpose they have in mind when they do it. In the law firm we studied, we found that attorneys who focused on the collective benefits of making connections ("support my firm" and "help my clients") rather than on personal ones ("support or help my career") felt more authentic and less dirty while networking, were more likely to network, and had more billable hours as a result.

Any work activity becomes more attractive when it's linked to a higher goal. So frame your networking in those terms. We've seen this approach help female executives overcome their discomfort about pursuing relationships with journalists and publicists. When we remind them that women's voices are underrepresented in business and that the media attention that would result from their building stronger networks might help counter gender bias, their deep-seated reluctance often subsides.

Andrea Stairs, managing director of eBay Canada, had just such a change in perspective. "I had to get over the feeling that it would be self-centered and unseemly to put myself out there in the media," she told us. "I realized that my visibility is actually good for my company and for the image of women in the business world in general. Seeing my media presence as a way to support my colleagues and other professional women freed me to take action and embrace connections I didn't formerly cultivate."

Many if not most of us are ambivalent about networking. We know that it's critical to our professional success, yet we find it taxing and often distasteful. These strategies can help you overcome your aversion. By shifting to a promotion mindset, identifying and exploring shared interests, expanding your view of what you have to offer, and motivating yourself with a higher purpose, you'll become more excited about and effective at building relationships that bear fruit for everyone.

Francesca Gino is a behavioral scientist and the Tandon Family Professor of Business Administration at Harvard Business School. She is the author of *Rebel Talent: Why It Pays to Break the Rules at Work and in Life* and *Sidetracked: Why Our Decisions Get Derailed, and How We Can Stick to the Plan.* **Maryam Kouchaki** is an associate professor of management and organizations at Northwestern University's Kellogg School of Management. Her research focuses on decision-making and ethics. **Tiziana Casciaro** is a professor of organizational behavior and HR management and holds the Marcel Desautels Chair in Integrative Thinking at the University of Toronto's Rotman School of Management. She is the coauthor of *Power, for All: How It Really Works and Why It's Everyone's Business.*

CHAPTER 3

How Leaders Create and Use Networks

by Herminia Ibarra and Mark Hunter

For two years, we followed a cohort of 30 managers making their way through what we call the leadership transition, an inflection point in their careers that challenges them to rethink both themselves and their roles. In the process, we found that networking—creating a fabric of personal contacts who will provide support, feedback, insight, resources, and information—is simultaneously one of the most self-evident and one of the most dreaded developmental challenges that aspiring leaders must address.

Adapted from an article in *Harvard Business Review*, January 2007 (product #R0701C).

Their discomfort is understandable. Typically, managers rise through the ranks by dint of a strong command of the technical elements of their jobs and a nose-to-the-grindstone focus on accomplishing their teams' objectives. When challenged to move beyond their functional specialties and address strategic issues facing the overall business, many managers do not immediately grasp that this will involve relational—not analytical—tasks. Nor do they easily understand that exchanges and interactions with a diverse array of current and potential stakeholders are not distractions from their "real work" but are actually at the heart of their new leadership roles.

A majority of the managers we work with say that they find networking insincere or manipulative—at best, an elegant way of using people. Not surprisingly, for every manager who instinctively constructs and maintains a useful network, we see several who struggle to overcome this innate resistance. Yet the alternative to networking is to fail—either in reaching for a leadership position or in succeeding at it.

Watching our emerging leaders approach this daunting task, we discovered that three distinct but interdependent forms of networking—*operational, personal,* and *strategic*—played a vital role in their transitions. The first helped them manage current internal responsibilities, the second boosted their personal development, and the third opened their eyes to new business directions and the stakeholders they would need to enlist. While our managers differed in how well they pursued operational and personal networking, we discovered that almost all of them underutilized strategic networking. In this article, we describe key features of each networking

TABLE 3-1

The three forms of networking

Managers who think they are adept at networking are often operating only at an operational or personal level. Effective leaders learn to employ networks for strategic purposes.

	Operational	Personal	Strategic
Purpose	Getting work done efficiently; maintaining the capacities and functions required of the group.	Enhancing personal and professional development; providing referrals to useful information and contacts.	Figuring out future priorities and challenges; getting stakeholder support for them.
Location and temporal orientation	Contacts are mostly internal and oriented toward current demands.	Contacts are mostly external and oriented toward current interests and future potential interests.	Contacts are internal and external and oriented toward the future.
Players and recruitment	Key contacts are relatively nondiscretionary; they are prescribed mostly by the task and organizational structure, so it is very clear who is relevant.	Key contacts are mostly discretionary; it is not always clear who is relevant.	Key contacts follow from the strategic context and the organizational environment, but specific membership is discretionary: it is not always clear who is relevant.
Network attributes and key behaviors	Depth: building strong working relationships.	Breadth: reaching out to contacts who can make referrals.	Leverage: creating inside-outside links.

form (summarized in table 3-1, "The three forms of net-working") and, using our managers' experiences, explain how a three-pronged networking strategy can become part and parcel of a new leader's development plan.

Operational Networking

All managers need to build good working relation-ships with the people who can help them do their jobs. The number and breadth of people involved can be impressive—such operational networks include not only direct reports and superiors but also peers within an operational unit, other internal players with the power to block or support a project, and key outsiders such as suppliers, distributors, and customers. The purpose of this type of networking is to ensure coordination and co-operation among people who have to know and trust one another in order to accomplish their immediate tasks. That isn't always easy, but it is relatively straightforward, because the task provides focus and a clear criterion for membership in the network: Either you're necessary to the job and helping to get it done, or you're not.

Although operational networking was the form that came most naturally to the managers we studied, nearly every one had important blind spots regarding people and groups they depended on to make things happen. In one case, Alistair, an accounting manager who worked in an entrepreneurial firm with several hundred employ-ees, was suddenly promoted by the company's founder to financial director and given a seat on the board. He was both the youngest and the least-experienced board member, and his instinctive response to these new responsibilities was to reestablish his functional credentials. Acting on a hint from the founder that the company might go public, Alistair undertook a reorganization of the accounting department that would enable the books to withstand close scrutiny. Alistair succeeded brilliantly in upgrading his team's capabilities, but he missed the fact that only a minority of the seven-person board shared the founder's ambition. A year into Alistair's tenure, discussion about whether to take the company public polarized the board, and he discovered that all that time cleaning up the books might have been better spent sounding out his codirectors.

One of the problems with an exclusive reliance on operational networks is that they are usually geared toward meeting objectives as assigned, not toward asking the strategic question, "What *should* we be doing?" By the same token, managers do not exercise as much personal choice in assembling operational relationships as they do in weaving personal and strategic networks, because to a large extent the right relationships are prescribed by the job and organizational structure. Thus, most operational networking occurs within an organization, and ties are determined in large part by routine, short-term demands. Relationships formed with outsiders, such as board members, customers, and regulators, are directly task-related and tend to be bound and constrained by demands determined at a higher level. Of course, an individual manager can choose to deepen and develop the ties to different extents, and all managers exercise discretion over who gets priority attention. It's the quality of relationships—the rapport and mutual trust—that gives an operational network its power. Nonetheless, the substantial constraints on network membership mean these connections are unlikely to deliver value to managers beyond assistance with the task at hand.

The typical manager in our group was more concerned with sustaining cooperation within the existing network than with building relationships to face nonroutine or unforeseen challenges. But as a manager moves into a leadership role, his or her network must reorient itself externally and toward the future.

Personal Networking

We observed that once aspiring leaders like Alistair awaken to the dangers of an excessively internal focus, they begin to seek kindred spirits outside their organizations. Simultaneously, they become aware of the limitations of their social skills, such as a lack of knowledge about professional domains beyond their own, which makes it difficult for them to find common ground with people outside their usual circles. Through professional associations, alumni groups, clubs, and personal interest communities, managers gain new perspectives that allow them to advance in their careers. This is what we mean by personal networking.

Many of the managers we study question why they should spend precious time on an activity so indirectly related to the work at hand. Why widen one's circle of casual acquaintances when there isn't time even for urgent tasks? The answer is that these contacts provide important referrals, information, and, often, developmental support such as coaching and mentoring. A newly appointed factory director, for example, faced with a turnaround-or-close-down situation that was paralyzing his staff, joined a business organization—and through it met a lawyer who became his counsel in the turnaround. Buoyed by his success, he networked within his company's headquarters in search of someone who had dealt with a similar crisis. Eventually, he found two mentors.

A personal network can also be a safe space for personal development and as such can provide a foundation for strategic networking. The experience of Timothy, a principal in a midsize software company, is a good example. Like his father, Timothy stuttered. When he had the opportunity to prepare for meetings, his stutter was not an issue, but spontaneous encounters inside and outside the company were dreadfully painful. To solve this problem, he began accepting at least two invitations per week to the social gatherings he had assiduously ignored before. Before each event, he asked who else had been invited and did background research on the other guests so that he could initiate conversations. The hardest part, he said, was "getting through the door." Once inside, his interest in the conversations helped him forget himself and master his stutter. As his stutter diminished, he also applied himself to networking across his company, whereas previously he had taken refuge in his technical expertise. Like Timothy, several of our emerging leaders successfully used personal networking as a relatively safe way to expose problems and seek insight into solutions— safe, that is, compared with strategic networking, in which the stakes are far higher.

Personal networks are largely external, made up of discretionary links to people with whom we have something in common. As a result, what makes a personal network powerful is its referral potential. According to the famous six degrees of separation principle, our personal contacts are valuable to the extent that they help us reach, in as few connections as possible, the far-off person who has the information we need.

Watching managers struggle to widen their professional relationships in ways that feel both natural and legitimate to them, we repeatedly saw them shift their time and energy from operational to personal networking. For people who have rarely looked outside their organizations, this is an important first step, one that fosters a deeper understanding of themselves and the environments in which they move. Ultimately, however, personal networking alone won't propel managers through the leadership transition. Aspiring leaders may find people who awaken new interests but fail to become comfortable with the power players at the level above them. Or they may achieve new influence within a professional community but fail to harness those ties in the service of organizational goals. That's why managers who know they need to develop their networking skills, and make a real effort to do so, nonetheless may end up feeling like they have wasted their time and energy. As we'll see, personal networking will not help a manager through the leadership transition unless he or she learns how to bring those connections to bear on organizational strategy.

Strategic Networking

When managers begin the delicate transition from functional manager to business leader, they must start to concern themselves with broad strategic issues. Lateral and vertical relationships with other functional and business unit managers—all people outside their immediate control—become a lifeline for figuring out how their own contributions fit into the big picture. Thus strategic networking plugs the aspiring leader into a set of relationships and information sources that collectively embody the power to achieve personal and organizational goals.

Operating beside players with diverse affiliations, backgrounds, objectives, and incentives requires a manager to formulate business rather than functional objectives and to work through the coalitions and networks needed to sell ideas and compete for resources. Consider Sophie, a manager who, after rising steadily through the ranks in logistics and distribution, was stupefied to learn that the CEO was considering a radical reorganization of her function that would strip her of some responsibilities. Rewarded to date for incremental annual improvements, she had failed to notice shifting priorities in the wider market and the resulting internal shuffle for resources and power at the higher levels of her company. Although she had built a loyal, high-performing team, she had few relationships outside her group to help her anticipate the new imperatives, let alone give her ideas about how to respond. After she argued that distribution issues were her purview, and failed to be persuasive, she hired consultants to help her prepare a counterproposal. But Sophie's boss simply concluded that she lacked a broad, longer-term business perspective. Frustrated, Sophie contemplated leaving the company. Only after some patient coaching from a senior manager did she understand that she had to get out of her unit and start talking to opinion leaders inside and outside the company to form a sellable plan for the future.

What differentiates a leader from a manager, research tells us, is the ability to figure out where to go and to enlist the people and groups necessary to get there. Recruiting stakeholders, lining up allies and sympathizers, diagnosing the political landscape, and brokering conversations among unconnected parties are all part of a leader's job. As they step up to the leadership transition, some managers accept their growing dependence on others and seek to transform it into mutual influence. Others dismiss such work as "political" and, as a result, undermine their ability to advance their goals.

Several of the participants in our sample chose the latter approach, justifying their choice as a matter of personal values and integrity. In one case, Jody, who managed a department in a large company under what she described as "dysfunctional" leadership, refused even to try to activate her extensive network within the firm when internal adversaries took over key functions of her unit. When we asked her why she didn't seek help from anyone in the organization to stop this coup, she replied that she refused to play "stupid political games. . . . You can only do what you think is the ethical and right thing from your perspective." Stupid or not, those games cost her the respect and support of her direct reports and coworkers, who hesitated to follow someone they perceived as unwilling to defend herself. Eventually she had no choice but to leave.

The key to a good strategic network is leverage: the ability to marshal information, support, and resources from one sector of a network to achieve results in another. Strategic networkers use indirect influence, convincing one person in the network to get someone else, who is not in the network, to take a needed action. Moreover, strategic networkers don't just influence their relational environment; they shape it in their own image by moving and hiring subordinates, changing suppliers and sources of financing, lobbying to place allies in peer positions, and even restructuring their boards to create networks favorable to their business goals. Jody abjured such tactics, but her adversaries did not.

Strategic networking can be difficult for emerging leaders because it absorbs a significant amount of the time and energy that managers usually devote to meeting their many operational demands. This is one reason why many managers drop their strategic networking precisely when they need it most: when their units are in trouble and only outside support can rescue them. The trick is not to hide in the operational network but to develop it into a more strategic one.

One manager we studied, for example, used lateral and functional contacts throughout his firm to resolve tensions with his boss that resulted from substantial differences in style and strategic approaches between the two. Tied down in operational chores at a distant location, the manager had lost contact with headquarters. He resolved the situation by simultaneously obliging his direct reports to take on more of the local management effort and sending messages through his network that would help bring him back into the loop with the boss.

Operational, personal, and strategic networks are not mutually exclusive. One manager we studied used his personal passion, hunting, to meet people from professions as diverse as stonemasonry and household moving. Almost none of these hunting friends had anything to do with his work in the consumer electronics industry, yet they all had to deal with one of his own daily concerns: customer relations. Hearing about their problems and techniques allowed him to view his own from a different perspective and helped him define principles that he could test in his work. Ultimately, what began as a personal network of hunting partners became operationally and strategically valuable to this manager. The key was his ability to build inside-outside links for maximum leverage. But we've seen others who avoided networking, or failed at it, because they let interpersonal chemistry, not strategic needs, determine which relationships they cultivated.

———————

Herminia Ibarra is the Charles Handy Professor of Organizational Behavior at London Business School and the author of *Act Like a Leader, Think Like a Leader* (Harvard Business Review Press, 2015). Follow her on Twitter @HerminiaIbarra and visit herminiaibarra.com. **Mark Lee Hunter** is an adjunct professor at INSEAD and a cofounder of the Stakeholder Media Project at the INSEAD Social Innovation Center.

CHAPTER 4

How to Create Your Own Career Luck

by Christian Busch

Job seekers, entrepreneurs, and executives aiming to advance their careers need to nurture *serendipity:* the unexpected good luck resulting from unplanned moments, in which proactive decisions lead to positive outcomes.

How can we cultivate this "smart luck"? By *setting hooks* and *planting bombs.* These two practices can help us flex our serendipity muscles at any time. Here's how to deploy them.

Adapted from content posted on hbr.org, August 24, 2020 (product #H05TAB).

Setting Hooks

Serendipity hooks help people get interested in you and help you learn what you'll find intriguing about them. The process starts when you use memorable or engaging talking points, whether in the park or on Zoom. When Oli Barrett, a London-based entrepreneur, meets new people, he sets several hooks aimed at surfacing overlaps with the other person. If asked, "What do you do?" he will say something like, "I love connecting people, have been active in the education sector, and recently started thinking about philosophy, but what I really enjoy is playing the piano." That reply includes four hooks: a passion (connecting people), a vocation (education), an interest (philosophy), and a hobby (playing the piano). If he merely responded, "I'm in education," the potential for others to connect the dots would be quite small. But by setting several hooks, he increases the odds that the listener will respond with something like: "What a coincidence! I'm thinking about starting a company that is all about connecting people. Let's talk!" Hooks allow others to find and latch onto something that relates to their lives or what they're looking for, making serendipity more likely. Setting them is easier if we have our story straight: What are we passionate about, and what could we contribute that is relevant to the other person?

We can also give others the opportunity to set hooks. One way is to ask questions differently and be open to unexpected answers. Imagine being at a conference and meeting a new person. Try using a broad opener, such as "What are you interested in at the moment?" or "What is your state of mind?" Such prompts may lead to serendipitous outcomes by allowing the other person to set one or more of their own hooks.

Hook setting isn't limited to private conversations. We can set hooks at events, even if we're not the speaker—for example, by standing up during a Q&A and saying something like: "Thank you for the inspiring presentation. As someone who just went through [XYZ period] or who aspires to do [XYZ activity], I was struck by what you said about [XYZ topic]. What would you advise people like me to do?" This gives the entire audience insight into how you and your life and career might relate to theirs. In my experience, in a group of a couple hundred people, usually several will respond to such hooks by seeking out the person who set them: "What a coincidence! I recently went through [XYZ] as well. . . ."

Planting Bombs

Through technology and spatial design, it's possible to create entire containers of potential opportunity—what Mattan Griffel, an entrepreneur and adjunct assistant professor at Columbia University, calls *serendipity bombs*—by connecting with groups of people.

One tactic is to write speculative emails to people you admire. I know executives who do this, and you'd be surprised at how often the recipients of those unsolicited correspondences write back because they see some unexpected mutual interests or reasons to engage. For example, an executive might have wanted to expand into exactly the area that a speculative email referred to. If you can't find an email address, consider tweeting, direct messaging, or using LinkedIn's InMail function. In many professional fields, academics are a good starting point for making connections. Their contact details tend to be on their university's homepage, they usually know senior people in industry, and they are relatively open to making introductions. Even with all the background information available to us with just a few keystrokes, we can't know everything about a person, so you're creating new opportunities when you plant this type of bomb. It's a low-risk strategy to expand your network and nurture the conditions for serendipity. Even if nothing comes of it immediately, you are on your correspondent's radar.

You can plant serendipity bombs within organizations, too. One traditional way is to invite someone in a different department or function to coffee or a video call. Leaders might pair people up randomly to get unexpected conversations started. Our research has shown that companies and incubators have developed a myriad of similar ways, such as conducting postmortems (incentivizing people to share ideas that did not work out, which might work out in other contexts) and using flexible space design (for example, placing the mailboxes of diverse people next to one another so that those people will bump into one another) to increase serendipity, especially in the context of uncertainty.

Most top executives will admit that they've achieved their position through not just intelligence and hard work but also luck. Still, we can all do a better job of creating unexpected opportunities and connecting the dots with others so that they can help us or we can help them. With a serendipity mindset, every interaction might open a new path—for finding love, meeting an investor, making a friend, forging a new interest, or landing a new job.

———————

Christian Busch teaches on purpose-driven leadership, innovation, and entrepreneurship at New York University (NYU) and at the London School of Economics (LSE). At NYU, he directs the CGA Global Economy Program. Previously, he codirected the LSE's Innovation and Co-Creation Lab and cofounded the Sandbox Network as well as Leaders on Purpose. He is the author of *The Serendipity Mindset: The Art and Science of Good Luck.*

Great First Impressions

CHAPTER 5

Eight Questions to Ask Someone Other Than "What Do You Do?"

by David Burkus

We've all been in the awkward situation of meeting someone new and having to build rapport quickly—at networking events, industry conferences, charity events, dinner parties, and other social-professional situations. If you're like many people—especially most Americans— you break the awkward silence with a pretty standard question: "So, what do you do?"

Adapted from content posted on hbr.org, January 30, 2018 (product #H044LZ).

But that question might not be the best way to build rapport with someone else. In fact, it may be best to avoid talking about work entirely.

Research findings from the world of network science and psychology suggest that we tend to prefer and seek out relationships where there is more than one context for connecting with the other person. Sociologists refer to these as *multiplex ties*, connections where there is an overlap of roles or affiliations from a different social context. If a colleague at work sits on the same non-profit board as you or sits next to you in spin class at the local gym, then you two share a multiplex tie. We may prefer relationships with multiplex ties because, research suggests, such relationships tend to be richer, more trusting, and longer-lasting. We see this in our everyday lives: The work friend who is also a "friend" is far more likely to stick with you should one of you change jobs. And it goes the other way, too: People who have at least one real friend at work report liking their jobs more.

Which brings us back to the problem of using "So, what do you do?" as your opener.

Assuming you're already at a work-related networking event or meeting another person in a work context, the question quickly sets a boundary around the conversation that the other person is now a "work" contact. It's possible you might discover another commonality and build a multiplex tie, but it's far less likely to happen in that conversation.

Instead, consider beginning your introductory questions with something deliberately non-work-related and trusting that the context of the meeting will eventually steer the conversation back to work-related topics. Toward that end, here are a few questions you could start with that will leave you more likely to find multiple commonalties and turn your new contact into a multiplex tie—and maybe even into a friend:

What excites you right now? This is a question that has a wide range of possible answers. It gives others the ability to give a work-related answer or talk about their kids, their new boat, or basically anything that excites them.

What are you looking forward to? This question works for the same reason but is more forward-looking than backward-looking, allowing others to choose from a bigger set of possible answers.

What's the best thing that happened to you this year? Similar to the previous two but reversed: more backward-looking than forward-looking. Regardless, it's an open-ended question that gives others a wealth of answers to choose from.

Where did you grow up? This question dives into others' backgrounds (but in a much less assertive and loaded way than "Where are you from?") and allows them to answer with simple details from childhood or to engage in their story of how they got to where they are right now and what they're doing.

What do you do for fun? This question steers the conversation away from work, unless of course they are lucky enough to do for work what they'd be doing for fun anyway. Even then, it's understood as a nonwork question, and the most likely answers will probably establish nonwork ties.

Who is your favorite superhero? This might seem random, but it's one of my favorites. Occasionally, asking this question has led me to bond over the shared love of a character, but more often you'll find a shared connection or two in the reasons why the other person chose that particular character . . . or why they're not really into superheroes.

Is there a charitable cause you support? Another big, open-ended question (assuming they support at least one charitable cause). It's important to define support as broader than financial donations, as support might be in the form of volunteering or just working to raise awareness. You're also really likely to either find shared ground or discover a cause you didn't know about.

What's the most important thing I should know about you? This one is effective for reasons similar to many of the above, plus it gives the broadest possible range from which they can choose. It can come off as a little forthright, so when to use it depends on a lot of contextual clues.

Regardless of which question you choose, the important thing is to ask a question open-ended enough to allow others to select nonwork answers if they choose. Doing so will increase the chances that you didn't just turn a stranger into a new contact on your phone but that you actually made a new friend.

———————————

David Burkus is an organizational psychologist and best-selling author of four books, including *Leading from Anywhere*.

FIND YOUR AUTHENTIC CURIOSITY

by Alyssa Westring

Whether you're networking at a cocktail party or sending a message over LinkedIn, one of the most common ways to make yourself feel awkward is to get in your own head about what to talk about. Fear of stilted small talk, long silences, or grammar mistakes can paralyze us from engaging.

Rather than trying to avoid these situations at all costs, I've found that refocusing your attention on curiosity can help quiet some of those fears. The good news? Most people love to talk about themselves, so if you approach them with curiosity, they're bound to feel pretty good about the interaction.

Before entering networking situations, take some time to ask yourself what you would really like to learn about this person and their experiences. Expressing genuine curiosity will allow the conversation to flow much more smoothly than if you're faking it. This might

(continued)

FIND YOUR AUTHENTIC CURIOSITY

mean doing a little bit of background research when preparing for a networking event.

You can read someone's bio or latest tweets or research an organization's mission and values—but do so with the goal of piquing your curiosity rather than memorizing the "right" questions to ask in order to make a good impression. It's a subtle mindset shift, but it can make a world of difference.

———

Alyssa F. Westring is the Vincent de Paul Professor of Management and Entrepreneurship at DePaul University's Driehaus College of Business. She is the coauthor of *Parents Who Lead* (Harvard Business Review Press, 2020).

Adapted from "The Awkward Person's Guide to Networking" on hbr.org, September 20, 2021.

CHAPTER 6

How to Perfect an Elevator Pitch About Yourself

by Daisy Dowling

You're in the elevator with the hiring manager of Dream-Job Corporation. As the door slides shut, you feel a combination of adrenaline and slight nausea: You've got 15 seconds, if that, to communicate your value as a potential employee in a compelling way—just 15 seconds to cram in a whole résumé's worth of work and accomplishments and late nights and successes. There's so much you want to say, but your message has got to be crisp, tailored, to the point. Handle this one right, and you'll

---

Adapted from content posted on hbr.org, May 4, 2009 (product #H0035K).

be the newest member of the Dream-Job team. Flub it, and you're back to scanning listings online and sending résumés into the ether. What are you supposed to say?

Here are the five key things to know and do in order to make your elevator pitch successful:

- **Practice, practice, practice.** Very few people have the oratorical power to make a compelling 15-second speech about their entire professional lives on demand and under pressure. Practice your speech 100 times—literally. Know it, get comfortable with it, be able to tilt it effectively for a different audience. Practice your body language with it: How will you give the speech differently sitting down versus while walking down a hall? How will it be different over the phone as opposed to in person?

- **Focus on impact.** Recently, I saw a TV segment about a white-collar job fair. One of the interviewees, a laid-off Wall Street executive assistant, looked straight into the camera and said, with total conviction, "I can make any boss shine." I wanted to hire her on the spot. Who doesn't want to shine? Describing the impact you've had, and can continue to have, is much more compelling than talking about your number of years of experience.

- **Ditch the cultural baggage.** A lot of us have been taught—by parents, teachers, or team-oriented corporate environments—not to toot our own horns and to use "we" instead of "I." Elevator pitches are all about "I." You've got to get comfortable with bragging about your own individual contributions (in a graceful way—see chapter 8).

- **Be slow and steady.** Whether out of nervousness or a desire to cram in a lot of information, people giving elevator speeches tend to talk at breakneck pace, which is extremely off-putting to potential employers. Speak at a pace that shows your calm and confidence. You want them to think of you as thoughtful and deliberate—not as some manic babbler.

- **See the whole world as an elevator.** Too many people looking for jobs save their elevator speeches for job fairs and interviews. Remember the first rule of sales: ABC (Always Be Closing). Give your elevator speech to everyone—at family gatherings, in the waiting room of the dentist, at coffee hour at your church or temple. You never know where the next job is coming from.

Daisy Dowling is the founder and CEO of Workparent, a specialty coaching and advisory firm focused on working parents. She is the author of *Workparent: The Complete Guide to Succeeding on the Job, Staying True to Yourself, and Raising Happy Kids* (Harvard Business Review Press, 2021).

CHAPTER 7

Three Ways to Pitch Yourself in 30 Seconds

by Jodi Glickman

People often think of the elevator pitch as something you use when you're interviewing for a new job or trying to raise capital for a new venture. The elevator pitch, however, is no less important once you've got the job than it is when you're looking.

In fact, your personal 30-second spiel about who you are, how you're different, and why you're memorable is arguably more important once you've landed that great position or won the support of investors and now

---

Adapted from content posted on hbr.org, October 8, 2009.

interact with senior colleagues and important clients regularly.

A managing director on Wall Street once told me of a summer associate who made an uncharacteristically strong impression on senior leadership during a welcoming cocktail party. Within days, the managing director received numerous calls from senior partners advising him to "make sure she gets the attention and resources she needs to succeed this summer." The young woman's career has been on the fast track ever since.

So what can you possibly say over canapés and white wine to create so many powerful advocates so quickly and effectively? Think through the following ideas before you craft your pitch:

1. Have a compelling reason for *why* you want to be there, as in "Why did you decide to join the firm?"

2. Know what it is that uniquely qualifies you for the position so that you can answer the *how*, as in "How did you actually get a job here?"

3. Be able to explain *what* ties together past and current experiences in a way that is compelling and makes sense: "What is the glue that holds your story together?"

Of course, no executive or senior manager would dare ask those questions. But your elevator pitch is your opportunity to communicate these critical pieces of information to someone in a crisp but casual way—without even being asked.

As you answer the why, how, and what:

1. **Think relevant, not recent.** There's no rule that says you must talk about your résumé in reverse chronological order. Mike was a marketing executive who took a sales position abroad for two years. Yet when he returned to marketing, he kept introducing himself as someone who had just made a career switch, always leading off with an anecdote about his short stint in sales. Instead, Mike should have started with the fact that he was a seasoned marketing professional who had taken a sabbatical but was now back where he belonged—putting his marketing prowess to work and thinking about what drives consumer spending habits.

2. **Focus on skills-based versus situation- or industry-based qualifications.** You don't have to have a background in finance to be good at finance. Alex was a chemist and researcher who had gone back to business school to get her MBA. She decided she wanted to work in corporate finance for a large pharmaceutical company, but she was afraid no one would take her seriously given her background. When I pressed Alex to explain to me why she chose finance, she exclaimed, "That's the way my brain works." Her thinking was methodical and mathematical—which translated to someone who was a natural fit within a corporate finance department. Instead of focusing on the fact that her

background was in academia, Alex could emphasize to colleagues and clients that she was a numbers person at her core.

3. **Connect the dots—what ties it all together?**
    Whether you are a chemist turned finance professional or a marketing executive with experience in international sales, you should find a way to bring together the richness of your experiences and show how each one complements the other. Personally, I had a significant hurdle to clear with clients as a former Peace Corps volunteer turned investment banker. I explained away the dichotomy of the two by emphasizing to others that I was big-picture thinker by nature and a numbers person by training. Banking was a perfect combination of the two—I liked looking at clients' challenges and issues from 30,000 feet and then digging down into the details to come up with creative financing solutions. Whether the client was the mayor of my Peace Corps town in Chile or the CEO of a health-care company, I could start at a high level and drill down quickly and effectively.

Here are sample pitches for all three situations:

Mike:
I'm a marketing executive. Because of my lifelong fascination with what drives consumer spending, I'm looking for a position in the retail industry. I recently took a two-year sabbatical in a sales role abroad,

which gave me some great international experience, but I belong in marketing, and I'm excited to be headed in that direction again.

Alex:

I'm really looking forward to combining my passions for finance and science and learning about the pharmaceutical industry. I come from academia, but corporate finance is a great fit for me—my mind is wired for math, and I'm highly methodical.

Jodi:

I'm not your typical investment banker—I actually spent five years in the public sector as a Peace Corps volunteer in Latin America and as a policy analyst at the EPA. But I'm a big-picture thinker by nature and a numbers person by training, so you're in good hands—banking is pretty much a perfect combination of the two.

Pitches like these pay off. Alex's, for instance, helped get her the pharma job she wanted. And mine helped me win clients' trust when I moved to investment banking. So carefully craft your own pitch—and create more opportunities for yourself.

————————

Jodi Glickman is a keynote speaker and the CEO of leadership development firm Great on the Job. She is the author of *Great on the Job*.

CHAPTER 8

The Right Way to Brag

by Francesca Gino

In both our social and professional interactions, we commonly focus on managing the impressions that others form of us, especially when these others do not know us well. In fact, when we first approach these situations and stakes are high, we often receive the same advice from colleagues, mentors, and friends: Try to make a good impression. Though this is generally good advice, our intuitions on what types of strategies will create a positive impression are often wrong.

While we are naturally nervous about revealing our weaknesses or outright bragging about our strengths,

---

Adapted from "The Right Way to Brag About Yourself" on hbr.org, May 20, 2015 (product #H022OX).

doing so often is more effective than saying things that could make us seem inauthentic or insincere. A case in point is "humblebragging," a particular type of self-promotion that, thanks to social media, has become ubiquitous. Here are some examples:

- "I find it incomprehensible that I'm booking my life past July of next year right now. It's too much!"

- "I have got to stop saying yes to every interview request. That last nine minutes felt like a week."

- "Graduating from two universities means you get double the calls asking for donations. So pushy and annoying!"

Humblebragging allows people to highlight positive aspects of their lives while attempting to appear modest by masking the "good news" as a complaint.

Consider one of the most common job interview questions, "What's your greatest weakness?" Think about the last time you asked this question or had to answer it. I bet that, depending on your role, you either heard or crafted an artful response that reframed something positive as a flaw: "I'm such a perfectionist that I drive myself crazy" or "I tend to work too hard, which can take a toll on my personal life."

People humblebrag to try to make a positive impression on others without appearing vain, but, as it turns out, humblebragging frequently fails. Research I conducted in collaboration with my Harvard Business School colleagues Ovul Sezer and Mike Norton shows that observers find the strategy insincere. Our findings suggest that showing we are self-aware and working on improving our performance may be a more effective strategy in job interviews than humblebragging. After all, authentic people who are willing to show vulnerability are likely to be the type of candidates interviewers most want to hire.

Even outside of interview contexts, humblebragging does not seem to produce the positive impressions we all hope for. In follow-up studies we found that people dislike humblebraggers more than braggers and even more than complainers. And the costs of humblebragging extend beyond interpersonal evaluations to affect behavior, causing people to penalize humblebraggers financially and be less likely to help them out.

What these results seem to suggest is that when deciding whether to (honestly) brag or (deceptively) humblebrag, would-be self-promoters should choose the former—and at least reap the rewards of seeming sincere.

More generally, authentic behavior can have unexpected rewards. In research I conducted with Sezer; Alison Wood Brooks, another Harvard Business School colleague; and Laura Huang of Wharton, we found that most people believe catering to another person's interests in professional and social interactions is more beneficial than just simply being oneself. This belief is wrong: People are evaluated more positively when they try to be themselves (see the following sidebar). This is because people experience greater anxiety and

BEING YOURSELF REALLY DOES WORK

by Francesca Gino

One common strategy for getting off on the right foot when networking is to try to learn the other person's expectations and interests and then tailor the conversation to them. Ovul Sezer and Alison Wood Brooks of Harvard Business School, Laura Huang of the Wharton School, and I conducted research to test whether this approach works. We found it doesn't.

We surveyed 458 working adults from a wide range of industries. Sixty-six percent of them said they would use this strategy—which we call "catering"—in high-stakes situations like first meetings, and 71% reported believing that it would be the most effective approach in the given situation. But we found that across different contexts, catering to another person's interests and expectations, as opposed to behaving authentically, harms performance. Why? Because when a person tries to anticipate and fulfill others' preferences, it increases his or her anxiety and feelings of inauthenticity.

The conclusion: Because feeling at ease can go a long way toward leaving a good impression when networking, simply being ourselves is a good solution to dealing with the anxiety and uncertainty of approaching others.

Adapted from "When Networking, Being Yourself Really Does Work" on hbr.org, September 27, 2016 (product #H035HA).

inauthenticity when they cater to another person's interests and expectations rather than being themselves.

In this research, we also explored the real-world implications of authenticity in a field study. We looked at entrepreneurs who pitched their ideas to potential investors. We found that catering to perceived expectations negatively influenced their evaluations (e.g., the likelihood of getting funded) while being oneself positively influenced them.

Together, these studies point to an important truth: Our intuition about what types of strategies will create a positive impression on others is often wrong. We believe that humblebragging will be more effective than simply bragging, when in fact it backfires. And we also believe that catering to others' interests and expectations will make us look good, when in fact simply being oneself delivers better results.

Francesca Gino is a behavioral scientist and the Tandon Family Professor of Business Administration at Harvard Business School. She is the author of *Rebel Talent: Why It Pays to Break the Rules at Work and in Life* and *Sidetracked: Why Our Decisions Get Derailed, and How We Can Stick to the Plan.*

Connecting at Conferences and Events

CHAPTER 9

How to Network Better at Conferences

by Rebecca Knight

In-person conferences are an overwhelming rush of presentations, conversations, and potential meetups, and it can be tough to know where to focus your time. How do you figure out which sessions to attend? Should you skip the keynote to meet an important contact? How many coffee dates are too many?

What the Experts Say

Even if you dread the multiday extravaganza of breakout talks and cocktail-infused networking sessions, you must

---

Adapted from "How to Get the Most Out of a Conference" on hbr.org, July 8, 2015 (product #H0274Q).

resist your impulse to stay home. Meeting people at conferences "who likely have the same interests as you and are highly relevant to your work" is a good way to nurture and expand your network, says Dorie Clark, a networking expert and author of *The Long Game*. "The fact that technology has made it easier to interact with people across great distances and time zones actually makes face-to-face interaction even more valuable." Here's how to get the most from the conferences you attend.

Pre-introduce yourself

Weeks before the conference starts, "think about the people you would really like to get to know and then carve out time to accomplish that goal," says Francesca Gino. Clark recommends creating a "priority wish list" of people you'd like to meet. Reach out to those people on LinkedIn or email introducing yourself; if possible, get an introduction from a mutual friend or colleague. If the person is presenting, tell them that "you're going to make it a point to come to their session," says Clark. "There's a lot of fear when presenting that no one will come to your session, so the fact that you're making the effort will be appreciated." If the person is not presenting, invite them for coffee. Or inquire "if there's any session they're excited about going to, then ask: 'Can we sit together?'"

Be strategic with your time

Consider two things when choosing which sessions to attend. "A session should fulfill either a content goal, meaning the talk will be educational, or it should fulfill an interpersonal goal, meaning you want to meet or support the person who is presenting," Clark says. The keynote speech is usually skippable, but because someone famous often delivers it, "it's fun to go," she adds. "It's likely to be entertaining and will give you bragging rights as in: 'Hey, I heard Elon Musk speak.'" That said, "the keynote doesn't have much networking value beyond being a conversation starter."

Network on your terms

If plunging into a crowd makes you uneasy, you've got to "take initiative to create a situation where you feel comfortable," says Clark. Perhaps one-on-one meetings are better for you or small group settings. If so, Clark suggests making a reservation at a local restaurant for about eight people before the conference. Then invite people from your wish list. "You want it to be a mix of people you know and people you would like to get to know better," says Clark. "Tell your invitees that you're bringing together a group of interesting people, and you'd like them to join." And be sure to tell them why the dinner is of interest. "If she's a tech entrepreneur, tell her that you're also inviting venture capitalists," for example.

Listen more; talk less

When you're attending a semiprofessional, semisocial networking situation—such as a group dinner or conference cocktail reception—your goal is to "allow enough space for others to shine," says Clark. Harness *quiet power* by asking thoughtful questions and *listening carefully* to how others respond. Having conversation starters at the ready can make small talk more palatable. For example, you might ask: "Which session are you most excited to attend?" If you've invited people together, it's also important that you "exert sufficient control" of the situation. "Make sure people are interacting with and getting to know each other," she says. Ask people to introduce themselves. Think of commonalities among group members and highlight those when you're making introductions. "Try to bolster group cohesion rather than letting it be a fragmented experience," says Clark.

Manage your existing connections

Conferences can be useful venues to solidify your current professional relationships. After all, says Gino, "good networking not only means creating new connections. It also means maintaining and strengthening existing ones." But don't spend all your time with people you already know. That defeats the purpose of going to the conference in the first place. "If you know beforehand that certain colleagues are likely to glom on to you, draw clear boundaries—for both of your sakes," says Clark. Having existing dinner or lunch plans can be handy. "Say to your colleague: 'I need to meet new people tonight, but tomorrow I'm going to a session that I think we'll both find interesting. Would you like to go together?'"

Make time for yourself

Conferences are exhausting, especially if you're not an extrovert. "The fundamental truth about being an introvert is that you need to manage your energy differently from other people," says Clark. "You need to know when you're on the brink." And so if you spend five days pushing yourself to attend every luncheon, cocktail party, and networking reception, "you're going to be worn out and frayed, and you will not be at your best." Put simply: Skip happy hour. In its place, do something restful or restorative. This is sound advice for both introverts and extroverts. "It's easy for any professional to lose sight of self-care" because he or she is busy, adds Clark. Eating well, exercising, and getting enough sleep are important to our health. Don't neglect your own well-being. One of the most important ways to do this, says Gino, is to try not to be someone else when you're in social situations. "Focus on being yourself," she says. "This will help ensure that you don't stress out too much or get too tired."

Case Study 1: Organize Small-Group Gatherings and Take Time to Recharge

Parisa Parsa, the executive director of the Public Conversations Project—a Boston-based group that helps workers and organizations create constructive dialog in their professional, civic, and personal lives—attends several conferences a year. "I don't know if I will ever figure out how to make conferences not exhausting," says Parsa, a natural introvert, "but I know what I need to do to make them productive."

Earlier this year, Parsa, who is also a minister, attended the annual Unitarian Universalist Association conference in Portland, Oregon. Before she arrived, Parsa reached out to several people with whom she wanted to connect at the conference and invited them for coffee or a meal. "I do terribly when it comes to chatting with people on the spot, so I tried to set up one-on-one meetings so I could focus my attention and not have to fight for airtime," she says. "Reaching out to people in advance made sure I was on their radar. They knew they were a priority to me."

In the past, she has also arranged small group dinners around specific topics. Since most people know her but don't necessarily know each other, Parsa gets the conversation flowing by asking everyone to introduce themselves and to provide an initial take on the topic at hand. "I like bringing people together for a smaller, structured gathering. Big groups can be overwhelming."

Parsa also makes sure to not wear herself out by giving herself time to rest and recharge. "I used to feel that I had to be at each and every session, but now I'm more strategic about choosing sessions based on the content."

During her most recent conference, she went for frequent walks around Portland and nipped into coffee shops to reflect on and write about the presentations she'd seen. "I tried to see a little bit of the city," says Parsa. "It's really sad when the only part of the city you remember is the inside of convention centers."

Case Study 2: Offer Your Assistance in Order to Be Seen as a Potential Resource

Ron D'Vari, CEO of New York–based advisory firm NewOak Capital, is a self-described "conference junkie" who attends dozens of conferences each year. Conferences, he says, "expose me to new ideas and perspectives and give me a sense of the marketplace and where things are going."

One year, after he learned about the upcoming Professional Risk Managers' International Association (PRMIA) conference in New York, the first thing he did—and what he always does—was call the conference organizer. "I asked if I could help with content—I volunteered to speak or to moderate a panel, and I let them know I could help introduce them to other speakers," says D'Vari. "Offering to be a part of the conference provides many more networking opportunities than merely attending the conference."

D'Vari won a spot on a panel. Before the conference started, he examined the agenda and looked at the list of speakers and presenters. Whenever he came across a person he wanted to meet, he sent them an introductory email and a request to connect on LinkedIn. "That way, they know who you are," he says.

D'Vari attended the conference with several colleagues, but he made sure to go to different sessions and networking events. "You can't stay in a clique with colleagues," he says. "It's time to get to know other people." After all, "conferences are expensive. You've got to be able to get your two grand's worth of connectivity."

When networking, D'Vari also makes an effort to do more listening than talking. "My objective is to be seen as a resource for people. I want to engage them in a way so that when they have a technical question down the road, they think to pick up the phone and call me."

At the PRMIA conference D'Vari made many connections, including with a Fed official with whom he is currently writing a paper.

Rebecca Knight is a senior correspondent at Insider covering careers and the workplace. Previously she was a freelance journalist and a lecturer at Wesleyan University. Her work has been published in the *New York Times*, *USA Today*, and the *Financial Times*.

CHAPTER 10

Tips for Navigating a Room Full of Strangers

by Amantha Imber

I hate the feeling of walking into a large conference hall and seeing a sea of strangers. Everyone seems to be having an amazing time, connecting with long-lost friends, whereas I feel like a social pariah. I'm always at a loss as to how I will infiltrate the crowd and find even one single person who might want to talk to me. If I do manage to find that person, I struggle with what to say. How do I keep the conversation going?

Adapted from "Easy Tips for the Networking Haters" on hbr.org, October 15, 2021.

I've interviewed many experts for my podcast, *How I Work*, and they've suggested some very interesting (and practical) ways to get your way around networking. Here's some advice on how to get better at it.

Look for Islands

Marissa King, professor of organizational behavior at the Yale School of Management and author of *Social Chemistry*, hates networking, yet, somewhat ironically, has dedicated more than 15 years to researching social networks.

"What we know from research is that people don't form walls or oceans. They actually tend to clump together in small groups," King told me. "So really, it's not an ocean of people; it's only little islands. Then the question is, 'Now that I know they're islands and things feel a bit more manageable, what am I going to do next?' What researchers have found is that people almost always interact in groups of two or dyads. It's really the most fundamental unit of human interaction."

Using her research, King has developed a tactic. When she looks at the islands of people before her at a networking event, she tries to spot a group of odd numbers. "It might be three, five, seven—it doesn't really matter. If there's an odd number of people, then there's someone who really isn't a part of the conversation, and they are likely looking for a conversational partner. And so that's a very basic strategy that has become critical for me to start to navigate a lot of the social anxiety I feel in these types of situations because it gives me direction."

Reconnecting Is Networking

More networking happens virtually since Covid-19 began, and King says there is extraordinary power in our existing networks. And arguably, the most impactful thing that most people can do to improve their network is to reinvigorate dormant ties. Dormant ties are people whom you might not have seen in two or three years.

Research led by Daniel Levin from Rutgers Business School examined the benefits of reaching out to dormant ties. The researchers asked people to make a list of 10 current connections and 10 people whom they haven't reached out to in two or three years. Participants were then asked to reach out to those people for advice or help with a project. Levin and his colleagues found that dormant ties were extraordinarily powerful in that they provided their connections with more creative ideas, and, more surprisingly, the trust within those relationships had endured.

King applied this research to design a ritual that she now does every Friday. "I write down the names of two or three dormant ties. And I reach out to them just to say, 'Hey, I'm thinking about you.' Sometimes, I will have an ask or something I'm hoping to get out of it, like feedback or a question. But mostly, it's just reconnecting. That, for me, has been both a source of great joy but it's also been extraordinarily helpful."

Before starting this ritual, King was hesitant. "I thought, 'Oh my God, isn't this going to be awkward?'" Turns out, it wasn't.

"The more you do it, the more you realize that this is actually great. It's also helpful for me to imagine myself being in the other person's shoes. So if I imagine I received this email, would I be happy to get it? And the answer is almost always yes."

Turn It into a Game

One person I connected with at a TED conference and then interviewed was Jerry Dischler, vice president of product management at Google. Being on the introverted side, he was looking for strategies to make meeting some of the world's most high-achieving strangers less intimidating.

Dischler ended up meeting someone at the conference who gave him a great idea. "This person was a self-declared introvert who did not seem introverted at all. I asked him, 'How do you do this?' And he said, 'I approach it like a video game, actually.' So he pretends to be an extroverted character in a video game and he scores points by talking to new people."

Turning something from being scary into being fun is an effective way to change behavior. Humans are motivated by feeling a sense of progress, and scoring points for meeting strangers is a clear way of achieving this progress (see the sidebar "Networking with a Growth Mindset").

In addition, the opportunity to score points distracts us from the fear and, at worst, paralysis that can come with the idea of having to introduce ourselves to people whom we have never spoken to before.

by Herminia Ibarra

Many people believe that networking comes easily for the extroverted and runs counter to a shy person's intrinsic nature. If they see themselves as lacking that innate talent, they don't invest because they don't believe effort will get them very far.

Stanford psychologist Carol Dweck has shown that people's basic beliefs about "nature versus nurture" when it comes to personal attributes like intelligence or leadership skill have important consequences for the amount of effort they will put into learning something that does not come naturally to them. People with "fixed" theories believe that capacities are essentially inborn; people with growth mindsets believe they can be developed over time.

As shown in an academic paper by Ko Kuwabara, Claudius Hildebrand, and Xi Zou, if you believe that networking is a skill you can develop, you are more likely to be motivated to improve it, work at it harder, and get better returns for your networking than someone with a fixed mindset.

———

Herminia Ibarra is the Charles Handy Professor of Organizational Behavior at London Business School and author of *Act Like a Leader, Think Like a Leader* (Harvard Business Review Press, 2015). Follow her on Twitter @HerminiaIbarra and visit herminiaibarra.com.

Adapted from "5 Misconceptions About Networking" on hbr.org, April 18, 2016 (product #H02TMD).

Don't Stress Yourself with Preparing for Small Talk

From the outside, you'd think Kevin Rose is supremely confident. He was an angel investor in Facebook, Twitter, and Square. He founded the social news site Digg and hosts one of the top-ranking podcasts in America, *The Kevin Rose Show*. Yet Rose describes himself as socially awkward. He also hates small talk and has come up with some strategies for avoiding it.

"I try to find something that is not small talk but is also a mutual kind of interest," Rose told me. "There's a bunch of wacky things that I'm into, and so when people say, 'What have you been up to lately?' or 'What's new?' I could respond with something like how I am trying to inoculate tree trunks to help grow lion's mane mushrooms. And typically, someone responds with, 'Wow, tell me more.' Or they will share one of their wacky interests with me. It's something that is fun to talk about versus just being like, 'Oh, the weather sucks.'"

Prior to events, Rose will spend time consciously thinking about the various activities he has been engaging in and which might be of interest to the type of people he will be meeting.

Finally, Rose has found that people typically have a book to recommend, which can be another great way to avoid small talk. "I always like to say to people that I'm looking for a new book to read. So I ask them, 'What's a book that you've read in the last six months that you're really excited about or you could share with me?' People typically have something they're pretty stoked on." This is also a great way to start a conversation on LinkedIn, for example, and when people respond to your post, you can use it to continue the conversation via messages or even take it offline.

Whether you are attending events in the real world or confined to the virtual realm, networking doesn't have to be scary or hard. Making just a few small changes can help you overcome your fears and get back out there in no time.

———————

Amantha Imber is the founder of the behavioral science consultancy Inventium and the host of *How I Work*, a podcast about the habits and rituals of the world's most successful people.

CHAPTER 11

How to Plan Your Own Networking Event

by Dorie Clark

While attending conferences or scheduling meetups are great ways to connect with others, an often overlooked (or avoided) approach is organizing a gathering yourself.

Hosting your own events enables you to build relationships more strategically than a conference or mixer typically allows, because you're controlling the guest list, and as the convener, you get credit for the connections your guests make with one another. It's also an excellent

---

Adapted from "How to Plan Your Own Networking Event (and Invite the Right People)" on hbr.org, January 9, 2019 (product #H04QGF).

way for introverts to level the playing field, ensuring your gathering takes place in the kind of calm, quiet environment where you do best. If you're looking for tips on hosting a video call, see the sidebar "How to Host a Virtual Networking Event" later in this chapter.

In the years prior to the Covid-19 crisis, I hosted dozens of networking dinners—usually about once a month. I've discovered it's both a rewarding way to connect with people and much easier than I initially expected: You don't need a special skill set, and the logistics don't have to be overwhelming.

The first question to ask, of course, is who to invite. Many people overthink this—*Will anyone accept my invitation? Will people get along? What's the right mix?*—searching for a perfect combination that doesn't exist. As a result, they sometimes give up on the idea of hosting, or throw together a random assortment of people and hope for the best. Clearly, neither is optimal.

Instead, if you're interested in organizing your own networking gathering, here are five strategies you can use to curate your attendees and bring a fascinating mix of people together.

Think About the Size of Your Gathering

Many people are so caught up in *who* to invite, they forget an equally critical question: How many? When organizing a dinner, for instance, I try never to invite more than 10 people. Above that number, it becomes hard to have a single "table conversation" and create a unified experience for attendees—the goal for at least part of the evening. If you're just getting started and aren't yet comfortable hosting, a smaller group—perhaps six or eight—may be optimal.

Decide If Your Event Will Have a Theme

One way to guarantee attendees have something to talk about is to convene guests who may not know each other but have something in common—for instance, they all attended your alma mater, they're all in the tech industry, or they're all women entrepreneurs. This isn't mandatory, however. I often organize miscellaneous "interesting people" dinners, because high-performing professionals often enjoy meeting people outside their profession. It's not every day that busy startup CEOs get to know comedians or art critics.

Think Carefully About the Mix

If you're going for a mixed group, it's essential that it is a *genuine* assortment, not simply a cluster of connected people and then a few outliers. A group where six people already know each other well and two haven't met anyone is a recipe for disaster, because the old pals will likely revert to inside jokes and private conversations, leaving out the newcomers. It's your responsibility to make sure everyone is on equal footing.

It's also important to consider people's personalities. Most attendees mix reasonably well, but if you have one friend who you know has a hard time with social interactions (they tend to dominate conversations or consistently vent too much about politics, etc.), go with your gut: Maybe they won't be the right fit for this group event. As a host—just as if you were moderating an event—your job is to create a great overall group dynamic. And while you can't control every variable, choosing guests wisely makes an enormous difference.

Consider Recruiting a Cohost

If you feel like you don't know enough people to invite, one solution is to find a cohost. Think about friends and colleagues who have a wide social network—these are the "connectors" in your life. Over the years, I've co-hosted with several friends, and we typically split up responsibility for the guest list: For a dinner gathering, I'll plan to invite four colleagues, and so will my cohost. This takes pressure off us at the event (there are two people who can make sure the conversation is moving smoothly and that the appetizers are appearing at the right time as well) and cross-pollinates our social networks, enabling us to meet new people.

Build Your List Using Previous Guests

Once you've hosted someone at a dinner gathering, they become an ambassador of sorts. They understand what the events are like, so they have a sense of who else would make a good attendee and be eager to attend. You can use this dynamic to fill subsequent dinners with interesting guests. Follow up with your guests afterward, asking if they have friends they think would enjoy attending in the future, and if they would introduce you. A related strategy is to host a dinner with people you already know reasonably well and ask each of them to by Dorie Clark and Alisa Cohn

When Covid-19 forced us into social distancing, virtual networking became the norm. We learned that virtual events can be just as valuable to keep connections active and spark new ones, especially among people who live far away from each other.

Prepare for the Event

Keep it small. Limit yourself to eight attendees (including you) to ensure participants have enough time to speak and interact. We usually schedule 90-minute sessions, which is a comfortable amount of time to facilitate meaningful conversations and to allow everyone to speak without feeling rushed.

Make logistics as easy as possible for your attendees. Once someone has agreed to attend, send them a calendar invite with a link to the video app you're using, and be sure to alert them if they need to download software in advance or if the event requires a password.

A few days before your call, send an introductory email. Include the names of the participants, one-sentence descriptions, and links to their LinkedIn profiles. Also share guidelines for what to expect. Your email can say something like, "We look forward to seeing you at our virtual cocktail gathering. We'll start right at 6 p.m., so please join on time. We'll spend around 60 to 90 minutes together, with a mix of introductions and structured conversation. We'll be joined by the great people below. Bring your own beverage!"

(continued)

During the Event

Make people feel comfortable. Greet them when they enter and provide guidance about what to expect—just like you would at an in-person cocktail party. About five minutes after your start time (to allow people time to join), get started with introductions.

Ask each person to spend two minutes introducing themselves with a mix of professional and personal information, such as a favorite hobby or passion. Model this so they get a sense of the appropriate length and tone. Then, as the host, you can choose a person and ask them to go next, rather than waiting for a volunteer.

Ask each participant to answer a specific question. As the host, it's your job to structure the conversation so it doesn't become dominated by a loquacious guest or go down a rabbit hole of politics or current events. Ask everyone to answer an open-ended questions such as one of the following to share a little bit about themselves:

- What is an interesting or fruitful way you're using your time lately?

- Tell us about a time you've been resilient.

- What are you enjoying most about your job right now, and why?

- What's something unexpected you've learned or done in the past month/year?

People may have some back-and-forth around the questions, which helps build the rapport of an in-person cocktail party—but make sure to manage the conversation as needed to bring it back to the main question until everyone has had their turn to share.

If there's remaining time, there may be a natural flow of conversation, or you can pose an additional question (or ask if anyone has a question they want to pose to the group). A virtual gathering isn't typically conducive to one-on-one interactions, but by keeping our gatherings small, we ensure everyone can participate in a lively group conversation.

Wrap it up on time. No matter how well the gathering is going, it's a good idea to consider ending it after 90 minutes. People generally tire more easily from video meetings than in-person gatherings. If everyone is having a great time, you can leave on a high note—and you or someone else can always gather the group again.

After the gathering, send a quick follow-up email with everyone cc'd, thanking them for coming and encouraging them to connect with each other one-on-one, if they'd like.

———

Alisa Cohn is an executive coach who specializes in work with *Fortune* 500 companies and prominent startups, including Google, Microsoft, DraftKings, Venmo, and Etsy. She is the author of *From Start-Up to Grown-Up*.

Adapted from "How to Host a Virtual Networking Event" on hbr.org, May 26, 2020 (product #H05MW1).

bring a "plus-one" who they think is interesting, or who fits the evening's theme ("bring a friend who's a fellow journalist/IP attorney/CMO").

Networking is essential for business success, yet only a small percentage of professionals actually make the effort to host events. Following the strategies above, you can bring people together and deepen professional relationships that may prove critical in the years to come.

———————

Dorie Clark is a marketing strategist and keynote speaker who teaches at Duke University's Fuqua School of Business and has been named one of the Top 50 business thinkers in the world by Thinkers50. Her latest book is *The Long Game: How to Be a Long-Term Thinker in a Short-Term World* (Harvard Business Review Press, 2021).

Networking to Land a Great Job

CHAPTER 12

How to Get the Most Out of an Informational Interview

by Rebecca Knight

When you're looking for a job or exploring a new career path, it's smart to go out on informational interviews. But what should you say when you're actually in one? Which questions will help you gain the most information? Are there any topics you should avoid? And how should you ask for more help if you need it?

Adapted from content posted on hbr.org, February 26, 2016 (product #H02P48).

What the Experts Say

John Lees, a UK-based career strategist and author of *The Success Code*, says that informational interviews "give you exposure—a way to get yourself known in the hidden job market," he says. "The visibility may put you straight onto a short list, even if a job isn't advertised." They can also be a great boost to your self-esteem. "You get to wear smart business clothes and visit places of work, which maintains your confidence levels in a job search," he explains. So whether you're actively trying to change roles or just exploring different professional paths, here are some tips on how to make the most of an informational interview.

Prepare and Practice

Informational interviews are, according to Dorie Clark, "a safe environment to ask questions." But that doesn't mean you should go in cold. After all, your goal is to come across in a way that inspires others to help you. So do your homework. Study up on industry lingo. Learn who the biggest players are. Be able to talk about the most important trends. You don't want to waste your expert's time asking Google-able questions. "You will come across as a more serious candidate if you are familiar with the jargon and vocabulary," says Clark. Lees concurs. "Showing that you've done your background research plants the idea of credibility in the other person's mind," he says. Work on your listening and conversation skills too. Lees suggests that you practice "asking great questions and conveying memorable energy" with "people who are easy to talk to, such as your family, your friends, and friends of friends."

Keep Your Introduction Short

"What frustrates busy people is when they agree to an informational interview, and then the person seeking advice spends 15 minutes talking about himself and his job search" instead of learning from them, says Lees. It's not a venue to practice your elevator pitch; it's a place to "absorb information and find stuff out." Clark suggests preparing a "brief, succinct explanation about yourself" that you can recite in three minutes max: "Here's my background, here's what I'm thinking, and I'd like your feedback." People can't help you unless they understand what you're looking for, but this part of the conversation should be brief.

Set the Tone

"You want to leave people with a positive impression and enough information to recommend you to others," says Lees. At the beginning of the interview, establish your relationship by revisiting how you were connected in the first place. "Ideally, this person has been warmly introduced to you"—perhaps you have a friend or colleague in common or you share an alma mater—so remind them, he says. It's also a good idea to state at the outset that "you're interested in talking to 10 or 15 industry experts" during your information-gathering phase. "That way, the person will start to process the fact that you are looking for additional sources early on. If you wait until the end to ask for other referrals, she might be caught off guard."

Ask about time constraints up front too, says Clark. "If, at the end of the time allotted, you're having a good conversation, say, 'I want to respect your time. I would love to keep talking, but if you need to go, I understand.' Prove you're a person of your word."

Think Like a Journalist

Prepare a list of informed, intelligent questions ahead of time, says Clark. "You don't necessarily need to stick to the script, but if you're unfocused and you haven't planned, you risk offending the person." Lees recommends approaching your interview like "an investigative journalist would." You're not cross-examining your expert, but you should "gently probe through curiosity, then listen." He suggests a framework of five questions along the lines of Daniel Porot's "Pie Method":

- How do you get into this line of work?

- What do you enjoy about it?

- What's not so great about it?

- What's changing in the sector?

- What kinds of people do well in this industry?

You can adapt these questions to your purposes; the idea is to help you "spot the roles and fields that match your skills and experience and give you an understanding of how top performers are described," says Lees.

Deliberately Test Your Hypotheses

Your mission is to grasp the reality of the industry and the job so you can begin to decide if it's right for you. So don't shy away from sensitive topics. "You want to hear about the underbelly," says Clark. She suggests questions "designed to elicit negative information," such as:

- What are the worst parts of your job?

- What didn't you know before you got into this industry that you wish someone had told you?

Some topics, such as money, may seem taboo but can be broached delicately. "Don't ask, 'How much money do you make?' Instead, say something like, 'I've done some research online, and it seems that the typical salary range is this,' so you're just asking for confirmation of public information," says Clark.

It's also OK to ask for advice on "how to position yourself" for a job in the industry by making your experience and skills sound relevant. She recommends phrasing your question like, "Based on what you know about my background, what do you see as my weaknesses? And what would I need to do to allay the concerns of a potential hiring manager?" If the feedback is negative, consider it valuable information but get second and third opinions. "One person's word is not gospel," she says. "You may *not* be qualified, but you also may have spoken to a stick-in-the-mud who discourages everyone. Don't let him limit your career options."

Follow Up with Gratitude, Not Demands

While thanking the person for their time via email is a must, Lees recommends also sending a handwritten note to express gratitude right after you meet. "It will help you be remembered," he says. Your thank-you letter needn't be flowery or overly effusive; instead, it should describe how the person was helpful to you and, ideally, that their guidance led to "a concrete outcome" in your job search.

Whatever you do, don't immediately ask for a favor, adds Clark. Not only is it "considered bad manners," but it's also practically "an ambush because you barely know the person." That said, "if, a couple of weeks later, a job opens up at the person's company, you can tell the person you're applying for it and ask if she has any quick thoughts on professional experiences you should play up in your cover letter. If she takes the ball and runs with it and offers to put in a good word for you, that's great. But do not ask for it."

Play the Long Game

The real purpose of informational interviews is to build relationships and "develop future allies, supporters, and champions," says Lees. So don't think of them as one-off meetings in which "someone gives you 15 minutes of his time." Take the long view and think about ways to cultivate your new professional connection. Forward him a link to a relevant magazine article, for instance, or invite her to an upcoming conference or networking event. In other words, be helpful. "You want to be seen as giving, not constantly taking," Lees says. Clark notes that it can be a tricky proposition when there's a wide age or professional gap between you, but if you focus on keeping the person "apprised of your progress"—perhaps writing him a note saying you read the book he suggested or that you

joined the professional association he recommended—
"it shows you listened and that his advice mattered."

Case Study 1: Prepare and Be Gracious

Two years ago, Matt McConnell, who lives in southern California, wanted to move from finance to marketing. He wasn't entirely sure of his direction, so he began using informational interviews to learn about other people's careers in the hopes of narrowing his focus. "I was also using the interviews to learn more about other organizations to see whether they might be places I'd want to work," he says.

His first informational interview didn't go very well, and Matt takes full responsibility. "I didn't prepare," he recalls. "He could tell, and he told me that I was wasting his time."

Matt learned an important lesson. "I've never made that mistake again. I now always overprepare," he says.

To get ready, he reads people's LinkedIn profiles, does a Google search on their careers, and checks out their company's website. He tends to ask the same questions, usually in the realm of how the person got started and how they ended up in their current role. "But I also make notes about particular questions I want to ask so that I have something to reference if the conversation stalls," he says.

Matt also has a post-meeting routine. "I ask for a business card and immediately send a handwritten thank-you note. The thank-you is typically three lines long, and I always mention one specific thing from our meeting that resonated with me so they know I was listening and found their time valuable," he says.

"Early on in my career I worried that I didn't have anything to offer anyone in return. [But] I learned that people enjoyed sharing their experiences and offering advice, so I make sure to communicate my sincere gratitude."

Matt eventually had an informational interview with a marketing head of a quick-service restaurant group that yielded results. "After our meeting, the person called me and said her company was hiring for a role she thought I'd be perfect for," he says. "She'd given my name to the HR department, and they were planning on calling me within the next 30 minutes to do a phone interview. That phone interview led to in-person interviews and eventually a job offer at that company."

He worked at the company for a few years before moving on. He's now the marketing manager for Astrophysics, a company that designs X-ray scanners for security screenings.

Case Study 2: Be Respectful and Don't Let Negative Feedback Discourage You

A couple of years ago, Susan Peppercorn, a career coach and founder of Boston-based Positive Workplace Partners, decided she wanted to write a book about work satisfaction. Trouble was, she had no experience in the publishing industry beyond blogging. To educate herself, she did a lot of informational interviews.

"Some are with writers, others editors, and others published authors," she says. "In each case, I think in advance about each person's expertise and focus my questions on the areas where I think they might have the most valuable advice."

Susan made sure she was respectful of the other person's time, never asking for more than 30 minutes and always meeting at the person's convenience, not hers. Before each interview, Susan also considered how she might help the person with whom she's meeting: She might have a contact she could introduce, for instance, or she could offer to look over a résumé or cover letter.

One of her interviews was with a potential editor. Susan was excited, and she prepared by thinking about what this particular person would look for in taking on a client. She began the conversation with a two-minute description of her book idea. But during the discussion, it became apparent that the editor's goals and hers were quite different. "He told me in a very nice way that I had virtually no chance of having a publisher accept my book proposal. My balloon was burst quickly."

Still, after the initial disappointment, she found value in his advice. "I learned about the importance of having a platform before approaching a publisher, since they want to know in advance that your book will sell well," she says. "That saved me a lot of time and effort trying to pitch to publishers and helped me look at the viability of self-publishing. It also made me realize that I had more work to do with regard to clarifying and communicating the value of my book."

The experience also helped her hone her approach for subsequent informational interviews. She learned to share a brief outline of her book in advance, with a short paragraph on her motivation for wanting to write it.

A later meeting with a published author was extremely helpful. "He explained the concept of a platform and helped me brainstorm potential ones for my work," she explains.

Susan's work paid off—in 2018, she successfully published her first book, *Ditch Your Inner Critic at Work.*

Rebecca Knight is currently a senior correspondent at Insider covering careers and the workplace. Previously she was a freelance journalist and a lecturer at Wesleyan University. Her work has been published in the *New York Times*, *USA Today*, and the *Financial Times*.

CHAPTER 13

How to Reach Out to a Recruiter

by Marlo Lyons

Recruiters are your best friends when they see you as a potential fit for a job. They also can be as elusive as a yeti when you're trying to get their attention because *you* believe you're the perfect fit for a job.

We usually think of recruiters as people who reach out to potential candidates, not the other way around. But in periods of great job growth and churn, recruiters can't hire fast enough. If they're that busy, how can you get their attention—and when should you try? Here are three steps to approaching a recruiter in a way that's mutually beneficial.

Adapted from content posted on hbr.org, December 3, 2021 (product #H06Q2G).

Step 1: Know How Recruiters Work

A recruiter's job is to understand each role deeply enough to (a) find the right skills and capabilities for a job they've likely never done themselves, and (b) sell you on the position so you'll accept an offer if you're the best final candidate. Recruiters are part salesperson, part cheerleader, part coach, part therapist, and part strategist to both candidates and hiring managers.

Now picture a recruiter doing all that for multiple job openings at once. Let's say they have five viable candidates per job opening and are managing 10 openings. Yes: Most recruiters are managing more than 50 candidates at a time, some of whom may be passive candidates who need convincing to consider new opportunities. If recruiters responded to every random inquiry, they wouldn't have time to fill jobs. That's why it's so critical to reach out to them with a targeted approach.

Step 2: Know What Type of Recruiter You're Targeting

You need to understand exactly which type of recruiter— internal, external, or executive—you're reaching out to and what types of roles they recruit for so you can position yourself properly.

Internal recruiters

Internal recruiters are assigned to a specific area of their company—for example, engineering, marketing, finance, etc. So, if you reach out to a finance recruiter for a marketing job, you'll most likely be ignored. Also, a referral from a current employee or someone who knows the recruiter will garner more attention than a generic email. Internal recruiters don't tend to have databases of past candidates, so you should keep their name and email in case you find another applicable job at their company.

External recruiters

External recruiters don't work for the company with the job opening; instead, they specialize in specific business areas. For example, some external recruiters only recruit lawyers, while some specialize in industries like entertainment. Many external recruiters don't get paid if they don't find the candidate who ultimately accepts the job. In some instances, they may be competing with an internal recruiter who's also working to fill a role, and if the internal recruiter finds a top candidate, you may lose out if you're the external recruiter's candidate. But don't ignore external recruiters—many are hired because an internal recruiter has exhausted their search and needs an expert in the field. External recruiters generally do keep databases of candidates because they may be recruiting for similar roles at numerous companies.

Executive recruiters

Executive recruiters can be internal or external and mostly recruit for VP-level and higher roles. They do a lot of sourcing for the right candidate and may even seek candidates for confidential roles that aren't posted publicly.

Step 3: Know How to Approach a Recruiter

This is the most critical step. Never approach recruiters asking them to help you. They don't know you and you aren't paying them! Their job isn't to help you; your job is to help them do their job and fill roles. Approach a recruiter only after you've done your research, your LinkedIn profile and résumé are updated, you're ready to interview, and you understand whether the recruiter is internal or external and what types of roles they recruit for.

There are two reasons to approach a recruiter.

You can help them fill a current opening

If you can't see the name of the recruiter who posted a particular job, search LinkedIn using the name of the company plus the word "recruiter" or "sourcer," then read through recruiter profiles to determine their areas of focus. If you can find the one who recruits for the field you're interested in, you'll have a better chance of receiving a response to an inquiry.

Include the job opening you're interested in, provide the link to the online posting, describe your applicable skills and capabilities, and describe what value you can bring to the role and company using keywords from the job description. For example:

Hi [Recruiter Name],

I'm reaching out to you directly to express my enthusiasm about the [job opening/link] at [company name]. My extensive experience in [industry or skill] combined with my [hard/soft skills] and unique ability to [unique applicable skill] would make me a tremendous asset to [company name] in this role.

I hope you will seriously consider me for this position and give me an opportunity to explain further how I can bring outside-the-box value to the company.

Thank you,
[Your Name]

If you could be right for the role, you may receive a response. If you don't receive a response, it could be a matter of bad timing (i.e., the job may be close to being filled), or you're not as right for the role as you think you are.

You're certain the recruiter recruits for a specific industry and function

In this instance, you don't know if the recruiter is recruiting for any specific role, but you do know the types of roles and industries they specialize in. If the recruiter has a position you could fill now, then you may receive a response. Otherwise, they may enter your information into their database for when there's an applicable opening. So, make it easy for them to figure out which roles may be applicable:

Hi [Recruiter Name],

I'm reaching out because I am in the market for a new opportunity, and I understand you recruit for [types of roles]. Here is the type of role where I can bring the most value:

Position—Full-time employee. Open to contract work with conversion potential.

Title—Director, senior director, or VP of brand or consumer marketing, B2C.

Location—Greater DC area, no farther west than Fairfax County or east than Prince George's County. Open to relocation to West Coast.

Industries—Technology, SaaS, AI, cybersecurity, cryptocurrency, med-tech. Not interested in ride-sharing/self-driving auto companies.

Company—Prefer startups to under 5,000 employees but open for the right opportunity.

Compensation—Negotiable, minimum $100K total comp including equity. Must provide equity.

My résumé is attached for your review and my LinkedIn profile can be found here [link]. I look forward to hearing from you when you have a position where you think I could bring the most value.

Best,
[Your Name]

Finally, it's important to keep in mind that all recruiters want to fill job openings quickly and with the right people, but they don't work for you—they work for companies. They are the gateway, not the roadblock, to you securing your next role. If you help them do their job, then you're not only helping make them successful, but you may also land your dream role.

Marlo Lyons is a certified career coach and strategist, HR executive, and the author of *Wanted -> A New Career.*

CHAPTER 14

How to Find a Great Job Using the Strength of Your Weak Ties

by Claudio Fernández-Aráoz

The landmark research on how people find good jobs was conducted in the early 1970s by Mark Granovetter and remains relevant today despite the big changes in roles and recruitment that we've seen since. Studying professional, technical, and managerial job seekers, Granovetter found that most jobs (and especially good ones) were attained not through direct application or other formal

---

Adapted from "How to Find a (Great) Job During a Downturn" on hbr.org, June 15, 2020 (product #H05OA4).

means—that is submitting a résumé in response to a listing (which then might have been a print ad but is now online)—but through "personal contacts," who told the applicant about the position or recommended him or her to someone inside the organization.

Job seekers preferred this approach, noting that they got (and were able to give) better information during the process. Those who secured employment also benefited from higher pay, on average, and were more likely to be "very satisfied" in their roles, some of which, they reported, were even custom-created to suit their skills, knowledge, and experience. Based on more than 30 years of executive search experience, I'm convinced that most employers also prefer to work this way.

It's critical to understand which of your personal contacts are the most useful though. Granovetter also found that you're more likely to find jobs through personal contacts who are *not* too close to you, speak to you infrequently, and work in occupations different from your own. He captured this notion in a wonderful expression—"the strength of weak ties"—and many other researchers have since confirmed that diverse personal networks are the best way to find a new job. These acquaintances might come from your neighborhood, college, high school, fraternal organizations, or sports, recreational, or hobby groups; they might even be people you met once on vacation. In my view, activating these connections is the *only* job-seeking strategy that will allow you to secure a *great* position in truly tough times, though you must go about it in a disciplined way. Here's how.

Creating Your Contact List

During my first 20 years as a search consultant, I tried to find time each day to help one person who was either without a job or keen for a new one. This made for some 4,000 meetings with job seekers, many of which I conducted in Argentina, as its economy was in deep turmoil. In 2001, for example, it suffered the largest sovereign debt default in world history, and annualized GDP fell by 30% coupled with a 300% currency devaluation. My advice during those daunting days: Come up with a list of 100 (yes, *one hundred!*) weak ties without making any contact. The rationale? First, simple statistics: The probability of any one person leading you to the perfect job will be very low, so you have to tap many to improve your odds. Second and even more important: Because of the "weak" nature of these contacts, it won't be immediately obvious who can be most helpful. When you work to expand the list, you add quite unexpected people, including some truly great ones. Natural candidates for your weak-ties list include consultants, lawyers, auditors, suppliers, clients, as well as former bosses, colleagues, and professors, and so on. Some will be potential employers; others, sources. Look for ties in sectors that are likely to be stronger than most in the coming years and in which you would really like to work.

Next, rank everyone you've listed based on two factors: the attractiveness of the possibilities they can offer (given their company, role, and connections) and their willingness to help you (which depends on the quality of your relationship, even if it was limited or distant).

Making Connections

You might assume that I would tell you to first contact the person at the very top of the list. But I won't. Instead, start with number 10 or so. You will be nervous, tight, even shy at the beginning, and you will make mistakes. So gain confidence with a few lower-stakes conversations, and then start contacting your most promising targets. Make sure to rapidly cover the top 30 or so, ideally within a period of no more than a week or two. (If you're lucky enough to find more than one job possibility, it would be ideal to consider all of them at once.)

Of course, each conversation will be different depending on the person, opportunity, and previous relationship. But, with everyone, be candid about your reason for calling, the type of role you're looking for, and what you have to offer. People who have had a positive experience working with you will most likely want to help you, but they can't if they are unaware of or unclear on your need and aspirations.

Closing the List

In deciding when to end this process, you can make two types of mistakes: If you contact too few ties, you might not find any opportunities. If you contact too many, you might waste precious time on less attractive possibilities that will prevent you from properly focusing on the best ones. The key is to stop the calls when you have enough leads to give you a significant chance of landing a job. Consider, for example, that, as a result of your disciplined list-making and contact process, you are down to three potential employers. You estimate you have a 50% shot at getting the first job, 40% for the second, and 30% for the third. The probability of getting at least one offer can be easily calculated as one minus the product of the complementary probabilities, or $1 - (.5 \times .6 \times .7) = 79\%$. If you'd prefer to be 90% certain of getting a job, you'll need to keep calling prospects.

How do you go about estimating these probabilities? Simply use your judgment. If you were one out of three finalists in a search, your chances of landing that job would be one-third, or 33%. On the other hand, some leads might be so weak that only one out of 50 would turn into an offer, a probability of 2%. You should not eliminate these cases at this stage, though! If you contact 100 prospects with a 2% individual chance, the probability of getting at least one offer comes out at 87%, since $1 - .98^{100} = 87\%$.

Make your best estimate in each case, and don't worry too much about precision at this stage. Once you start getting answers (or not) from each of your contacts, these probabilities will start moving up (when there's mutual interest) or down. In the end most of them will turn to zero, while just a few will become significant. I've developed a downloadable support tool to help you track this.[1]

Managing Leads

At this point, you will hopefully have several leads. To keep all those balls in the air, even as you reach out to more of your targets, you'll need to proactively follow up on every promising conversation, including contacting new people that your weak ties have recommended you try. This can feel daunting! But, again, the support tool can help. It is a fully automated Excel spreadsheet, which includes a series of intuitive macro commands to easily sort leads by name, status (sources or potential employers), company, pending actions and deadlines, probability of receiving an offer, and priority. It will also automatically calculate the compounded probability of getting at least one offer so that you can more objectively decide when to move from lead generation to closure.

Sealing the Deal

As you talk to potential employers, you'll of course want to follow all standard job-seeking advice. Before you share your résumé, make sure you have updated it and that it stands out. When interviewing—which at this stage is likely to happen virtually—refresh yourself on best practices. Be able to answer open-ended prompts or behavioral prompts like, "Tell me about yourself" or "Tell me about a time when you overcame conflict/led a large team/had to collaborate across silos/managed a change initiative." Prepare and practice, including finding a quiet room with good lighting, and keep in mind the special challenges of virtual interviewing.

Remember to think carefully about your own priorities, preferences, and broader purpose and match them up against all the opportunities. Keep updating the spreadsheet with probabilities and new to-dos as the discussions progress. For your top priorities, create a strong list of references and let those people know that employers might be calling about you. Research the organization and its target markets. And, as venture capitalist Jeff Bussgang advises, come bearing gifts, such as proposals or project help, that show your commitment and work product.

A Composite Case Study

Let's consider the case of Juana, a character I've drawn from several professionals with whom I've worked. Born in the United States to working-class parents who emigrated from Mexico, she got her first job while in high school, working at a well-known fast-food franchise. By 19, she was the manager of a restaurant and pursuing her bachelor's degree in accounting. After graduation, she joined a Big Three consulting firm, earned her CPA, and rapidly advanced from analyst to manager in a few years. In November 2019, she accepted an offer from one of her clients, a global hotel chain, to join the company and lead its global HR analytics projects. Then the Covid-19 crisis hit. Eventually, Juana's project was canceled, and, on January 25, 2021, she was laid off. As a mother to two little girls, sharing responsibility for a mortgage and aging parents with her husband, she needed a new job. She spent the next week compiling a list of contacts. On February 1, she sent 20 emails to the most obvious sources and potential employers: a few managers and colleagues from the consulting firm, some former professors, an uncle, and several college classmates. She estimated that her probability of getting an offer from each ranged from 10% for her most recent boss at the consulting firm to 2% for most of the contacts. As can be seen in the screen capture on page 129, the compounded probability of getting at least one offer from this first group was just 55%.

So, on February 5, Juana emailed 15 more people on her list, including several former bosses from the fast-food franchise, all her former clients at the consulting firm, and a few additional personal connections. This included one to Pablo Rodríguez, a former HR leader for Latin America at the fast-food company, whom she had met just once at the company's worldwide convention when she won an award for best restaurant managers. While Juana received no response from most of the contacts she emailed, a dozen replied, including a former manager who was interested in her joining his electronic retail startup (to which she assigned a 40% probability of getting an offer), another manager interested in bringing her back (35% chance), and three other significant leads.

On page 130 you can see what Juana's process spreadsheet looked like by February 12.

Having reached a compounded probability of 93% of getting a job, Juana decided it was time to move from lead generation to closure. On page 131 you can see that she sorted the opportunities by priority rather than probability.

The job she thought she'd be most likely to get, a role at the electronic retail startup, was attractive because of her experience working with its founder and its potential financial upside; however, it would be a risky venture, with long and demanding hours. A job at her former consulting firm was second-most likely to come to fruition. She liked the company and her colleagues, but its policy was to put her back into her previous role at the

JOB SEARCH TOOL

P (At Least 1 Offer) = 55%

| Sort | Sort | Sort | Sort | Sort | Sort | Sort | Sort | Sort | Sort | Sort |
| 35 | 35 | 0 | 0 | 0 | 35 | 0 | 0 | 35 | 0 | 35 |
LAST NAME	NAME	PRIORITY	NEXT ACTION	DEADLINE	CONTACT	INTERVIEW	SOURCE	COMPANY	EMPLOYER	P(Offer)
Jones	Peter				1-Feb-21			eretail Startup		10%
Camara	Joao				1-Feb-21			College		5%
Hubler	Eric				1-Feb-21			Former Client		5%
Westley	Casey				1-Feb-21			Consulting Firm		5%
Gunninghan	John				1-Feb-21			Consulting Firm		2%
Miles	Fiona				1-Feb-21			College		2%
O'Brian	Caroline				1-Feb-21			Consulting Firm		2%
Other	Other				1-Feb-21			College		2%
Other	Other				1-Feb-21			College		2%
Other	Other				1-Feb-21			College		2%
Other	Other				1-Feb-21			College		2%
Other	Other				1-Feb-21			College		2%
Other	Other				1-Feb-21			College		2%
Other	Other				1-Feb-21			Fast Food Franch.		2%
Other	Other				1-Feb-21			Fast Food Franch.		2%
Other	Other				1-Feb-21			Former Client		2%
Other	Other				1-Feb-21			Former Client		2%
Other	Other				1-Feb-21			Former Client		2%
Other	Other				1-Feb-21			Uncle		2%

JOB SEARCH TOOL

| | | | P (At Least 1 Offer) = | | 93% |

Sort	Sort	Sort	Sort	Sort		Sort	Sort	Sort	Sort	Sort
35		8	8	8	35	3	0	35	10	35
LAST NAME	NAME	PRIORITY	NEXT ACTION	DEADLINE	CONTACT	INTERVIEW	SOURCE	COMPANY	EMPLOYER	P(Offer)
Jones	Peter	4	Discussion Pay	25-Feb-21	1-Feb-21	15-Feb-21		eretail Startup	1	40%
Smith	Brenda	3	Final Interview	1-Mar-21	1-Feb-21	24-Feb-21		Consulting Firm	1	35%
Rodriguez	Pablo	1	Deep Discussion	5-Mar-21	5-Feb-21	18-Feb-21		College	1	30%
Hubler	Eric	4	Discussion	5-Mar-21	1-Feb-21			Former Client	1	25%
Camara	Joao	5	Check Location	10-Mar-21	1-Feb-21			College	1	20%
Shakespeare	Joanna	3	Check Business	15-Mar-21	1-Feb-21			College	1	10%
Robbins	Sarah	2	Meet Partners	1-Mar-21	1-Feb-21			College	1	10%
Westley	Casey	2	Deep Zoom Call	20-Mar-21	1-Feb-21			Consulting Firm	1	5%
Wood	George	6			1-Feb-21			College	1	5%
Vasudeva	Sanjiv	6			1-Feb-21			Consulting Firm	1	5%
Gunninghan	John	6			1-Feb-21			Consulting Firm		2%
Miles	Fiona	6			1-Feb-21			College		2%
O'Brian	Caroline	6			1-Feb-21			Consulting Firm		2%

JOB SEARCH TOOL

P (At Least 1 Offer) = 93%

Sort		Sort	Sort	Sort	Sort	Sort	Sort	Sort	Sort	Sort
35		8	8	8	35	3	0	35	10	35
LAST NAME	NAME	PRIORITY	NEXT ACTION	DEADLINE	CONTACT	INTERVIEW	SOURCE	COMPANY	EMPLOYER	P(Offer)
Rodriguez	Pablo	1	Deep Discussion	5-Mar-21	5-Feb-21	18-Feb-21		College	1	30%
Robbins	Sarah	2	Meet Partners	1-Mar-21	1-Feb-21			College	1	10%
Westley	Casey	2	Deep Zoom Call	20-Mar-21	1-Feb-21			Consulting Firm	1	5%
Smith	Brenda	3	Final Interview	1-Mar-21	1-Feb-21	24-Feb-21		Consulting Firm	1	35%
Shakespeare	Joanna	3	Check Business	15-Mar-21	1-Feb-21			College	1	10%
Jones	Peter	4	Discussion Pay	25-Feb-21	1-Feb-21	15-Feb-21		eretail Startup	1	40%
Hubler	Eric	4	Discussion	5-Mar-21	1-Feb-21			Former Client	1	25%
Camara	Joao	5	Check Location	10-Mar-21	1-Feb-21			College	1	20%

same pay, and she wasn't sure she wanted to return to consulting work.

At the top of her ranking, surprisingly, was an alternative generated by Pablo Rodríguez, who had left the fast-food chain a few years earlier to join a 15-year-old rapidly expanding foundation with the purpose of helping poor, young high school graduates from Latin America prepare for, access, and persevere in quality jobs. He thought Juana could help him lead a digital transformation that would allow the organization to access a much larger population at a fraction of the cost, including to the U.S. Latino population. The role would pay less than the others but would allow her to work from home, reconnect with her roots, and give back to the Latin American community.

Confirming her strong interest in that job, Juana had several Zoom discussions with Pablo and the foundation's CEO and founder, did her own research on the needs of the young poor in Latin America and the U.S. Latino population, and prepared a detailed digital transformation plan. Her final interview was on February 18, and she nailed it. Three weeks after losing her job, she had a new one she could not feel more passionate about.

If you follow the process above it is not only possible but highly likely you will find a great job suited to your talents, purpose, and ambitions. It has helped the thousands of people I've advised through good times and bad, and I sincerely hope it also works beautifully for you!

NOTE

1. You can download the support tool at https://hbr.org/resources/pdfs/hbr-articles/2020/FernandezAraoz_JOB_SEARCH_TOOL.xlsm.

Claudio Fernández-Aráoz is an executive fellow for executive education at Harvard Business School and the author of *It's Not the How or the What but the Who* (Harvard Business Review Press, 2014).

Networking to Do Your Job Better

CHAPTER 15

The Best Way to Network in a New Job

by Rob Cross and Peter Gray

Anyone who hopes to hit the ground running in a new organization must first cultivate allies—a network of people who can provide the information, resources, and support needed to succeed. But few onboarding programs offer concrete advice on how to build those all-important connections.

Our research over the past decade shows that replicating the network of an established employee in a strong culture typically takes three to five years. But recently

---

Adapted from content posted on hbr.org, March 19, 2018 (product #H0485K).

we began to wonder if there was a way to accelerate that process. Could we develop a better blueprint for newcomer networking?

We started by tracking people joining companies with employee bases ranging from a few hundred to more than 40,000 people and pairing their progress in making social connections with monthly attrition data. The goal was to find newcomers who got connected (and productive) much more quickly than peers starting at the same time *and* who stayed in the organization through milestones, such as the first nine months and the two- to four-year tenure band, at which flight risk is greatest.

We found a few surprises. First, contrary to popular opinion, "brand building" across a very broad network was not necessarily better; in fact, it was correlated with departures in years two to four.

Successful newcomers were instead more selective and less superficial in their outreach. They still set up a lot of exploratory meetings, but they used them to ask plenty of questions, offer expertise and assistance where they were able, create mutual wins, and generate energy. Greg Pryor, head of talent at Workday, which partnered with us on this research, describes the difference as working to pull people into your network rather than pushing your way into theirs. "We teach our people how to draw people to their ideas and create energy in interactions from day one," he explains. "When you embrace the approach, you're much more likely to connect well."

We also found—again contrary to conventional wisdom—that newcomers do *not* need a strong tie to a formal mentor or leader in their first nine months.

More important for their long-term success was early contact with key opinion leaders—those well connected in the organization's networks, who were able to confer know-how and legitimacy—as well as to fellow newcomers, with whom they could form affinity groups.

Crucially, effective networkers also shift their strategy as they approach the two- to four-year time frame. They begin to streamline their interactions with close colleagues, resulting in collaborative demands that are 18% to 24% lower than their peers, while at the same time reaching across boundaries to connect with new people in different functions or divisions and those with similar values and passions, even when there is no clear short-term incentive to do so. The result for these networkers is more opportunities for enterprise-wide innovation and more sense of purpose in their work, which boosts their performance and engagement.

———————

Rob Cross is the Edward A. Madden Professor of Global Leadership at Babson College, founder of the Connected Commons, and the author of *Beyond Collaboration Overload* (Harvard Business Review Press, 2021). **Peter Gray** is a professor at the University of Virginia's McIntire School of Commerce and a senior editor at *Journal of the Association for Information Systems*.

CHAPTER 16

Start Networking with People Outside Your Industry

by Dorie Clark

Most professionals build a network over time through proximity—people from your business school study group, or colleagues from your current company or past jobs. You may have a few outliers in the mix, but unless you've been deliberate about your networking, the vast majority of people you know probably work in the same field or industry as you. It may seem innocuous,

Adapted from content posted on hbr.org, October 20, 2016 (product #H0377W).

but that inadvertent myopia can put you at serious professional risk.

First, if your network has become too narrow, you limit your options in case of a career change or a downturn in your company or industry. If coworkers are the only ones you know well, and you find yourself in the midst of layoffs, there's no one outside to turn to for assistance.

Additionally, you're more prone to groupthink if you're not exposed to diverse perspectives and points of view. As Harvard sociologist Robert Putnam has written, you need to have a balance of both "bonding capital" and "bridging capital"—that is, relationships based respectively on your commonalities (bonding) and relationships built across differences (bridging).

Dan, a senior professional I interviewed for my book *Reinventing You*, realized that he hadn't invested enough in his own bridging capital. He had spent a decade at a large technology company, rising to become an engineering director. But his entire professional network consisted of people from that company. Given the vagaries of industry disruption, he became concerned.

He embarked on a networking campaign that forced him to meet each week with people outside the company, including executive recruiters, venture capitalists, and startup entrepreneurs, among others. His connections allowed him to move to an exciting new job and immediately prove his value, thanks to the industry insights he'd gained from meeting with so many people.

To diversify your own network, here are four strategies you can follow.

- **Inventory your existing connections.** First, take an inventory of your current network. Who are the five to 10 people you spend the most time with? Next, make a list of your "outer circle"—the 50 or so people who matter the most in your professional life. Do a quick scan to evaluate the professional diversity of your network, noting whether they're inside or outside your company and whether they share your profession. If your network is weighted more than 70% in any direction (that is, 85% of your closest contacts are fellow marketers), it's time to think deliberately about how to diversify. Identify past colleagues whom you enjoy or friends who are in different fields or work at different companies but whom you haven't spent much time with. Take this as your cue to reach out and propose getting together; they'll often welcome the invitation.

- **Put networking on your schedule.** Part of Dan's success in broadening his network outside his company was his decision to make networking a deliberate part of his weekly routine. When he realized his circle had become dangerously small, he committed to regular breakfast meetings with new colleagues. Networking is never "urgent" and will often be the first activity jettisoned when things get busy at work, but it's essential to prioritize it by putting it on your schedule.

- **Ask for recommendations.** Almost everyone's network is overweight with people like themselves—

so take advantage of this fact and, as you're looking to diversify your professional relationships, ask the people who are outliers in your network to recommend people they think you should meet. You could say to them, "I'd like to know more angel investors, and you're really plugged into those circles—who else do you think I should connect with? Would you be willing to make an introduction?"

- **Don't look for immediate returns.** Some people end up with a narrow network because of inertia, but others don't extend themselves because they just don't see the potential for return. It's true that if you work in finance, making friends with a filmmaker is less likely to add to your bottom line than spending time with someone in your own industry. But you have to play the long game. People—including you—may change careers, and that connection may prove helpful down the line. Additionally, you can't predict who will be in someone else's network; that filmmaker may have gone to high school with someone you'd one day like to do business with.

The best reason to build a professionally diverse network, however, isn't about what you'll get out of those relationships. It's to fulfill personal curiosity and develop yourself as a person; professional or monetary ROI is a happy coincidence. It didn't seem relevant that one of my friends was a comedian and another a comedy promoter, until I started doing standup performances and was able to access helpful advice that saved me time and frustration.

It's easy to coast through life only connecting with people like ourselves—but by expending the extra effort to increase our bridging capital, we gain access to new insights and create more career insurance for ourselves by broadening the ranks of people who know, like, and respect our work.

———————

Dorie Clark is a marketing strategist and keynote speaker who teaches at Duke University's Fuqua School of Business and has been named one of the Top 50 business thinkers in the world by Thinkers50. Her latest book is *The Long Game: How to Be a Long-Term Thinker in a Short-Term World* (Harvard Business Review Press, 2021).

CHAPTER 17

Make Yourself Sponsor-Worthy

by Sylvia Ann Hewlett

"I've always given 110%," says Maggie. "Whoever I worked for, I gave them my all, every day, 10 hours a day, weekends and holidays, whatever it took. That endeared me to a lot of powerful men."

That dedication and loyalty should have made Maggie a star. Yet, although she rose in the organization, because she wasn't strategic about whom she gave her 110% to, she squandered her gifts on leaders who didn't invest in her. Without a sponsor to spotlight her attributes, offer her opportunities, and kick her career into high gear, she

---

Adapted from content posted on hbr.org, February 6, 2014 (product #H00NIB).

found herself stuck for years in what she calls "permanent lieutenant syndrome."

Maggie eventually was fortunate enough to find a sponsor and today is an executive at a global financial advisory firm with 22,000 people reporting to her. But there are thousands of Maggies out there—hardworking, devoted, consistent performers toiling in relative obscurity. If this sounds familiar, how can you break out of the pack and attract a sponsor?

Rather than hoping for a lucky break, focus your energies on making yourself sponsor-worthy. To begin with, you must come through on two obvious fronts: performance and loyalty.

When asked how she had built great relationships with three different sponsors, Sian McIntyre, head of Legal at Lloyd's Banking Group, says simply, "I've delivered." She hit her targets and deadlines, executed brilliantly on her assignments, and produced outstanding bottom-line results. "They all felt the benefit of that," McIntyre notes, "and wanted me on board for subsequent projects."

Loyalty manifests in many different ways: trust that's earned through repeated demonstration of a dedicated work ethic, commitment to a shared mission, and allegiance to the firm. Winning a sponsor's trust doesn't require becoming a toady. On the contrary, showing that you can ultimately be entrusted with a leadership position depends on demonstrating that you will stand up to him or her when necessary.

Tiger Tyagarajan, CEO of Genpact, attributes his success to the bond he cultivated with Pramod Bhasin, his boss and sponsor for 17 years. Because of a deep trust built on shared values, Bhasin would listen when Tyagarajan pushed back. "I'd say, 'Here's my logic on this,' and show him that I understood his logic but also show him why it wouldn't work. He was amenable to that as long as I kept it private," Tyagarajan recalls. "We had very different styles, and sometimes we simply agreed to disagree. But in the end, I think that what he valued in me was the very thing that complemented him."

But, as Maggie learned, performance and loyalty are not enough to get a sponsor's notice, let alone convince him to invest in you. You'll need to differentiate yourself from your peers. You'll need to develop and deploy a personal brand. You'll need to do *something* or be *someone* who can extend a sponsor's reach and influence by adding distinct value.

What do *you* bring to the table?

Some protégés add value through their technical expertise or social media savvy. Others derive an enduring identity through fluency in another language or culture. Consider acquiring skills that your job doesn't require but that set you apart—and make you a stronger contributor to a team. For example, in addition to his rapport with his boss, Tyagarajan had a special ability to build teams from scratch and coach raw talent—an invaluable asset that was key as the firm transitioned from a startup into a multinational info-tech giant. One 25-year-old sales rep, noting her potential sponsor "wasn't exactly current in terms of the internet," took pains to brief her on job candidates whose résumés bristled with technical jargon and references to social media innovation that she simply couldn't understand, let along assess for relevance. "I just helped educate her so she didn't come off as some kind of dinosaur," says the rep, whose tactful teaching gained her a powerful promoter.

Lastly, don't be shy about your successes. Alert potential sponsors to your valuable assets. Since it can be difficult to toot your own horn, work with peers to sing each other's praises. A VP at Merrill Lynch described how she and three other women, all high-potential leaders in different divisions of the firm, would meet monthly for lunch to update each other on their projects and accomplishments. The idea was to be ready to talk each other up, should an occasion arise. "So if my boss were to complain about some problem he's struggling to solve, I could say, 'You know, you should talk to Lisa in global equities, because she's had a lot of experience with that,'" this VP explained. "It turned out to be a really effective tactic, because we could be quite compelling about each other's accomplishments." In short order, all four women acquired sponsors and were promoted.

Finding the right person to highlight your accomplishments and push you to the top is a hard task, but it's necessary if you want to break out of the "permanent lieutenant" doldrums. Just doing good work isn't enough. Take the first step and make yourself not only a hard worker but an emerging leader worthy of a sponsor.

Sylvia Ann Hewlett is an economist, the CEO of Hewlett Consulting Partners, and the founder and chair emeritus of Coqual, formerly the Center for Talent Innovation. She is the author of 14 critically acclaimed books, including *Off-Ramps and On-Ramps*; *Forget a Mentor, Find a Sponsor*; *Executive Presence*; and *The Sponsor Effect*.

CHAPTER 18

How to Diversify Your Professional Network

by Amy Nauiokas

Diverse networks can foster new ways of thinking by connecting you to people whose viewpoints, insights, resources, and lived experiences differ from your own. People who are connected across heterogeneous groups and who have more-diverse contacts come up with more creative ideas and original solutions. Author Frans Johansson explores the idea of "intersectional thinking" in his book *The Medici Effect*, proposing that the best ideas emerge from the collision of different industry insights.

Adapted from content posted on hbr.org, August 29, 2018 (product #H04HOX).

Rethinking what it means to network, and acting accordingly, requires ongoing work and intention, as I've learned firsthand. Throughout my career—on Wall Street, in technology venture capital, and in media production—I've fostered a professional network that spans industries. Networking is central to my work as an investor and producer; it's my role to connect great people, identify partnerships, connect visionaries with resources, and cross-pollinate ideas.

Whether or not your daily work requires engaging with many different kinds of people, you can benefit from developing a network that inspires new ideas and challenges your beliefs. Here's my advice for making this shift.

Get Uncomfortable

Take a small step by meeting someone new and asking about the things you *don't* have in common. Try new experiences, especially ones you fear you're bad at. Trying something new could be as big as switching industries or as small as taking a dance class.

Make space in your day and in your list of priorities to expand what you think of as comfortable. If you need more accountability, write down specific goals. These could include things like spending two hours each week developing a skill that doesn't fit in with your current career path. (Remember, it was the calligraphy class Steve Jobs sat in on during college that later inspired Apple's typography.) You might ask five friends each month for introductions to people in their extended networks;

think about people at different levels and in completely different spaces.

I make a point to push myself beyond my comfort zone by saying yes to things that feel uncomfortable. Try it for one day (you'll have more time to do this if you also say no to other things).

Make Mindfulness Part of Your Networking Approach

There are a number of studies about the benefits of mindfulness for work performance and overall well-being, and mindfulness can extend to the way you approach networking. When you seek out meetings, brainstorming sessions, or even email exchanges with people outside your traditional work circle, it can be very inspiring. But it can also be difficult to put inspiration into action and process new ideas from so many different directions.

When your mind is quieter, you're in a better position to recognize when you're slipping into your comfort zone, so you can course-correct. You can also connect the dots between seemingly unrelated ideas, resulting in smarter solutions.

Seek Out "Collabotrarians"

At my organization, Anthemis, we've introduced "collabotrarian" groups—people from different roles, business units, and backgrounds (gender, race, ethnicity, age, thinking style) who come together to solve tough problems. The purpose of these groups is not to come to consensus. Instead, they serve as a space for healthy debate and divergent thinking, finding ways to reframe a problem and come up with multiple solutions, the best of which may not be obvious.

Create your own group by reaching out to people who think differently than you do and whose perspectives have been shaped by distinct experiences. You'll likely create these groups outside your office space and traditional career network, so a shared agenda or activity can give these meetings a greater sense of purpose. Unite people around a charitable cause completely different from their day-to-day roles. A monthly book or article club can give you the chance to hear the perspective of someone who doesn't share your opinion, as well as a chance to read authors you wouldn't normally pick up.

It is one of the ironies of our time that we have greater access to information but often find ourselves in echo chambers of people who share our opinions and worldviews. The digital age poses more opportunities than ever to carve out interesting, fulfilling careers by extending our networks beyond our comfort zones. So, let's go out of our way to get uncomfortable. Let's find the people who help to challenge our assumptions, call out our biases, and surface new ideas.

Amy Nauiokas is founder and president of Anthemis, a venture investment and financial advisory organization building a global network of entrepreneurs, financial institutions, academics, and policy makers.

Remote, Virtual, and Social Media Networking

CHAPTER 19

How to Tell Your Story on LinkedIn

by Alex Cooley

Your LinkedIn page is often the centerpiece of your online career persona, yet most of us barely consider what we're offering there. We serve up a motley buffet of achievements, experiences, identities, missions, and passions for readers to shovel through. Or we go the other way and set a sparse table with only the four basic food groups: name, current job, past experience, and education. The first approach overwhelms the reader—employer, investor, client, or ally—and the second leaves them starved for information and less likely to connect. The opportunity is lost, and we all go hungry.

Adapted from content posted on hbr.org, April 14, 2020 (product #H05IK9).

No matter how great you are in a role, if you can't articulate your value, it's that much harder to gain the sponsorship you need to move into the leadership positions you seek. With your LinkedIn page, it's essential to tell the story of your professional progression, lead your audience to its happy ending, and frame it in terms they care about. The result: You get the meetings, leads, and interviews that you actually want.

In my work as a career coach, I help midcareer women get hired, promoted, and buy-in for the impact they want to make. That means establishing a compelling leadership brand identity in the best, stickiest, and most effective way possible: by telling a cohesive and concise story that connects to the audience you want to reach most and getting them to reach out to you. To curate your LinkedIn page for storytelling success, follow these steps.

Write Your Own Happy Ending

Where is all your hard work leading? Are you the innovative CEO of a fast-growing company bent on bringing solar technology to every home along the Eastern Seaboard and then the world? Or the female diversity and inclusion evangelist who won't rest until half the CEOs of all *Fortune* 500 companies are women?

Knowing your professional story's bright, bold, happy ending anchors the narrative and helps you understand which pieces of your experiences, achievements, and results are relevant to your story.

Take Nichelle. For several years she'd been glued to her laptop, working 13-hour days, jumping every time her manager named a new height, all in the hopes of making director at one of the biggest social media platforms. But no luck.

All her efforts, words, thoughts, and writings were directed at that goal until we unpacked the true happy ending to her brand story: to become a content producer, writer, and speaker on matters of race. Because the skills and experiences of a writer or producer are vastly different from those of a marketing director, she needed to evaluate every line in her résumé, going over each skill she'd mastered, and boldly rewrite her internal dialogue and external communications to *only* include the parts that were relevant to her future as a speaker, writer, and maker concentrated on the experience of people of color.

Know Your Audience and Connect the Dots for Them

When you know your ending, you get a better sense of what your LinkedIn is for. Are you here to generate leads? Get the attention of recruiters? Make professional connections in your industry to move forward your vision? It's common to think that your LinkedIn should be about you. But as any brand strategist will inform you, every message is about positioning the product to meet the needs of its consumer. On your LinkedIn page, your mission is to present yourself so your partners, employers, sponsors, investors, or clients think, "This person has the answers I need!"

First step to doing that: Narrow who you're talking to and identify their needs.

Lila, who excelled in negotiations and business development, was a rising star at a tech company when she realized she wanted to pivot to working with content creators. After identifying that she wanted to work at a large, international firm with established premium content, we pulled out the similarities between her experience in selling premium consumer brands to millions of consumers and translated it to meet the needs of established content creators looking to sell premium shows to millions of viewers.

Two seemingly unrelated business focuses now flow from one to the other and create a seamless transition that any recruiter can understand immediately—and that Lila can reinforce in job interviews.

Look for Inspiration

With your future clear and your audience set, we can now move onto style. Despite what the internet might suggest, there is no one perfect template. Creating your leadership narrative on LinkedIn is a creative endeavor, so make like all great artists and steal, steal, steal.

Choose a LinkedIn profile or two that speak to you, and break down what's working and not working about yours as you see it and what you love about these other people's profiles. Frankenstein the exact pieces of their profile you love into your own draft to get a sense of the phrasing and order you might want.

This worked for my client Kiko when she moved from an operator to an investor in a venture fund she started. When it came time to advertise her new role on LinkedIn to companies she might invest in and investors she'd need to write her checks, she knew she needed to demonstrate strength, competency, and success in investing and operating, with hard data to back her claims.

By sending me a few LinkedIn profiles and articulating what she liked about each—the formatting of portfolio companies' successes, the tone, how people blended personal details into their professional summary—we crafted a hybrid profile that hit the right style while meeting her audience's needs and sealing her credibility.

Get to Work

With all the pieces in front of you, it's time to make this story your own. Keep what you love about your profile and ape other people's style, line by line if you want. If you love how someone tells a transformational story in their summary paragraph, go through each sentence of theirs and see how you could tell a similarly impactful story by swapping their details for yours. If you love how boldly someone describes their mission, try out your own. Even if it isn't perfectly worded, it's a start and definitely clearer than nothing, or what you had before. Remember, you can rewrite your LinkedIn.

You can have great dreams and the best experience to achieve them, but at some point you're going to need help from others. If you can't communicate what you want and instill confidence in others that you're the right person for that job, you're fighting an uphill battle with one arm tied behind your back and an eye patch. Developing a story around your leadership to suit your audience's needs is the first chapter of your gripping personal brand story. Spoiler alert: Learn how to use your

LinkedIn to tell a great story and you'll reach your vision faster.

_____

Alex Cooley is a former TV writer-producer (*The Colbert Report, Madam Secretary*) turned founder of ACElectric, a leadership storytelling consultancy for midcareer women in tech, media, and finance seeking promotion, that next-level role, and buy-in from their teams and bosses.

CHAPTER 20

What to Say When You're Reaching Out to Someone on LinkedIn

by Kristi DePaul

Sure, LinkedIn may lack the lighthearted user experience of other social platforms, but it's an essential tool for expanding your network. It offers the opportunity to track trends, make meaningful connections, and maintain a curated digital résumé that recruiters and potential employers can easily access and review.

If you've been hesitant to reach out to people on LinkedIn, or if you've been reaching out and not hearing

Adapted from content posted on hbr.org, November 2, 2020.

back, there are strategies you can use to increase your chances. But first, let's look at some common mistakes you might be making:

- **You don't know what you want.** Have you thought about why you're reaching out to someone? Are you seeking more information about a role or company? A relationship that can grow? Or a lifeline to a potential future mentor or employer?

- **You're putting your own needs first.** Don't be self-serving. No one will respond to "It would be good to connect with you," unless they know what's in it for them.

- **Your messages are weak.** Be specific and sensitive. Generic, nonpersonalized messages have a low probability of success. As entrepreneur Larry Kim has said: "What are the 11 most boring words in the English language? *I'd like to add you to my professional network on LinkedIn.*"

- **You're using an awkward tone.** Even the best messages may be met with silence or ghosting. Still, many continue to approach total strangers in a clumsier fashion than they'd ever dare in person.

- **You're not being persuasive enough.** If you haven't been able to convince the other person why you really want to connect with them, chances are they won't respond.

Now that you've identified what mistakes you're making, let's look at how you can overcome these and flip the odds in your favor. I recently reached out to experts, entrepreneurs, and authors who specialize in this area to learn more about formulating messages that both are authentic to your personal brand and will resonate with recipients at any level. Here's what they told me.

If You Are Seeking Advice on a Career Path or Job Change

People aren't employment oracles just waiting for your message soliciting their sage advice. Think deeply about the kind of guidance you want, and then identify the most relevant person to approach.

"Clarity is key when you're performing cold outreach," Cynthia Johnson, author of *Platform: The Art and Science of Personal Branding*, told me. "Assume that the person you're reaching out to is busy and wants to give you the best advice possible. If you're direct and specific as to what you're asking and why you're asking them, you will have created the perfect environment for a confident and thoughtful response."

Sending a vague (and all-too-common) "Can I pick your brain?" message isn't going to be helpful. Tim Herrera, founding editor of Smarter Living at the *New York Times*, recommends being straightforward and transparent to improve your chances of receiving a reply. "Whatever the ask is, the best favor you can do for yourself is not to beat around the bush. You're teeing the recipient up to give you exactly what you want because they know exactly what that is. You've taken away the ambiguity for them, which will save them time and mental effort, and you're also setting up the exchange to be as productive and efficient as possible." Of course, he added, you should always aim to be kind and courteous.

Here's an example of a note that is precise, but is flexible on timing:

> *Erica, your professional journey really stood out to me. I'm very interested in building my career as a [role]. Since you've been in that position, would you have some time to offer me a bit of advice on pursuing this? I would really appreciate a brief call at your convenience.*

If You Want Someone to Review Your Résumé or Cover Letter

When making this kind of request, put yourself in the shoes of the receiver and try to answer this question for them up front: Why is this person contacting me? Acknowledge that you're asking for a favor.

Here's a persuasive and considerate one that was sent my way:

> *Hi Kristi, you've built a really interesting career in thought leadership, and [mutual contact] mentioned you were a great resource as she revised her résumé. Since I'm hoping to advance from [my current role], I'd love to get your brief take on my cover letter if your schedule allows it.*

Receiving a carefully formulated request like this is somewhat rare, as it doesn't make any assumption that

I can provide a labor-intensive line edit to someone's application materials. Again, the acknowledgement that I'm using my time to help matters. In cases where I've been referred to job seekers by other people I've helped, I'm even more likely to respond. If someone I help then pays it forward by assisting others in their own circles, that makes the investment worth it. (In other words, always mention a referral if you have one.)

If You Are Inquiring About a Job Posting or Hiring Process

"We all have demanding schedules and are a little burned out," explained Amber Naslund, principal content consultant at LinkedIn—a role she landed after building a consistent presence on the platform. "Open-ended messages like, 'I just wondered if you had any openings . . .' aren't useful because all of those details are on a company's career page and that puts the work on the person you're asking."

According to Naslund, it's better to ask about a specific role and see if someone is willing to introduce you to a recruiter, make an internal referral, or answer questions you have about that role or the company. "Being respectful of people's time, expertise, and relationships can go a long way when you're trying to land your next job," she told me. The professional you reach out to could, for example, be a teammate who works closely with the role in question or the person who would be the immediate supervisor.

You could try a message like this:

Hi Cameron, I saw that your company is recruiting a marketing assistant. Since it seems you'd work directly with this person, it would be wonderful to hear your thoughts on the role. I'm looking to get some clarity on the role and responsibilities before I apply. Do you have a few minutes to speak with me about it in the next week or two?

If You Are Approaching a Potential Mentor

Before sending an invitation to connect, investigate whether or not someone might be interested in serving as a mentor.

Johnson recommends looking for a leader who demonstrates that they are both experienced in the areas in which you're seeking mentorship and show signs of having some availability.

Johnson found her longtime mentor on LinkedIn. "I assessed his expertise by doing diligent searches and thorough evaluations of his communications online with others." She identified the groups he had joined on the platform, including some where she noticed that he was very active, and joined them too. "His activity told me that he was interested in discussion and possibly had a bit of extra time to work with me," she said. "You can do this type of assessment, too, and find an amazing mentor."

When writing to a prospective mentor, make sure you've done your homework. Here's an example of a message you could send:

Divya, your posts on edtech in the STEM education forum have been really thought-provoking! I've interned for a few startups in this space and am excited about my own next steps—but I definitely could use some guidance from an experienced pro like you. Would you be open to chatting about this?

If You Are Reaching Out for Help After a Recent Job Loss

In need of others' assistance? Contextualizing your messages will make all the difference.

Job seekers should aim to strike up a conversation about their experience, what they're looking for, and who they feel might be helpful to them, Naslund said. "It's a great way to warm up the conversation and increase the likelihood that a new connection is willing to make some helpful introductions. People's networks are sacrosanct; most of us have worked very hard over a number of years to gain the trust of our networks and the people we've worked with, so we're not likely to open that up to just anyone and make cold introductions."

Here's an example of what you could say to let the other person know why you're reaching out to them:

Eitan, I'm looking to join a mission-driven team like yours and just happened to see your colleague's post about the product manager role. Would you be the right person to ask about one of the technical requirements? Let me know if I could send an email your way.

According to an old Chinese proverb, the best time to plant a tree was 20 years ago; the second-best time is now. So if you haven't cultivated your network, you'd better get started. But don't dive into a new relationship with a request straight away.

Andreas Klinger, a serial entrepreneur and investor in remote-first capital, recommends playing the long game. "Plan to have long-term engagement with someone (for example, in conversation via Twitter) well before you need anything. Or you can engage through content marketing—that is, sharing thoughtful articles on social media that you've written or admire—that will capture others' attention."

It's worth noting that if you want to connect with Klinger, paying attention to the preferred platform counts: In his LinkedIn profile, he advises that you reach out via Twitter. Others may also indicate the best way for you to contact them, which will up your chances of hearing back.

Now it's time to start putting these principles into practice. It's understandable that reaching out to people you've never met might feel intimidating—and that it means facing possible rejection. Try to remember that not only is rejection normal, it also indicates you're aiming high enough to achieve even greater success. Growth of any kind involves some risk. The advantage: You'll learn valuable lessons and can continually improve along the way.

———————————

Kristi DePaul is a writer, speaker, and global citizen who is passionate about technology and education as vehicles for upward social mobility and access to greater opportunities. She has written over 250 articles and blog posts on the remote-work landscape, and her work has been cited in research reports from international think tanks and universities. She is founder and principal at Nuanced, a thought-leadership firm focused on the future of learning and the future of work, and serves as CEO of Founders Marketing, a fully remote content-marketing company.

CHAPTER 21

The Best Ways to Use Social Media to Expand Your Network

by Doug Camplejohn

I'm a big believer in the power of social media to diversify and evolve one's network, build on the strength of weak ties, and nurture relationships over time. I've seen the business value of social media firsthand as the founder and CEO of three technology startups and as a product executive at LinkedIn. My experience is backed up by

Adapted from content posted on hbr.org, March 7, 2019 (product #H04TQW).

research: 75% of B2B buyers and 84% of executives use social media to make purchasing decisions, according to IDC. And LinkedIn's 2018 State of Sales report found that 89% of top salespeople consider networking platforms to be critical to closing deals.

That said, it can be challenging to reach out to people you don't know. I've been on the receiving end of sales pitches for the better part of 30 years, and I know how quickly online conversations can become transactional. But the more your interactions are modeled after genuine, in-person connections, the better. Here's my advice for building a stronger business network with the help of social media.

Don't Obsess About Seniority

Too many people focus on trying to network with senior people. Instead of reaching out only to executives, prioritize building relationships with your peers and with people who are earlier in their careers. This network will grow in seniority with you and connect you with opportunities down the line.

You're also more likely to get a response by looking beyond the C-suite. Our research at LinkedIn shows that response rates differ significantly by the seniority of the recipient. (LinkedIn applies machine learning to analyze aggregate data about the factors that influence message acceptance and reply rates.) People earlier in their careers respond most often to an initial message, while VPs and C-level professionals respond the least to people they don't already know.

LinkedIn InMail response rates relative to recipient's seniority

People earlier in their careers are more likely to respond to an initial message from someone they don't already know, while VPs and C-level professionals respond the least.

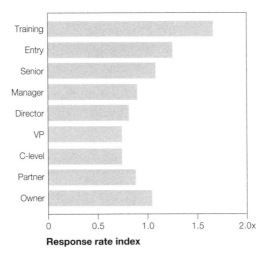

Response rate index

Source: LinkedIn, based on analysis of data from May 2014 to November 2018.

Be Brief But Personal in Your First Message

People don't have the patience to read long messages that look and feel spammy, especially if it's the first time they're hearing from you. I almost always ignore initial messages that are more than a paragraph. So, keep it brief—what are the three bullets you want to convey? Write those three sentences. Your entire message should be easy to read on a phone screen. Our InMail analysis found that messages under 100 words perform best, and response rates decrease significantly as word count increases beyond 500 words.

Of course, the content and tone of the message matters, too. The pros who get the best response rates treat their messages as handwritten notes with a personal touch. They let their voice come through and speak like a human. They also find common ground by referencing a common interest, a shared alma mater, or a mutual friend. According to our research, referencing a mutual connection boosts the acceptance rate of these messages by 51%, second only to attending the same school at the same time (53%).

Ask for Advice and Take Advantage of Transitions

There's an adage in fundraising that I learned as a startup founder: "If you go seeking advice, you get money; if you seek money, you get advice." Do the former. You wouldn't meet someone for coffee and start pitching them something, so don't do it online.

Often the best way to ask for advice is to be direct. It can be as simple as saying, "I'm kicking around some ideas and would love to bounce something off you. Can I buy you coffee?" or "I'm struggling with this problem and would really appreciate your insight. Do you have 15 minutes to talk?"

And if you're in a transitional period—starting at a new company, switching industries, or moving to a new city—recognize the opportunity to reach out to people, ask for their advice, and absorb their wisdom.

Pay It Forward

The best way to build a relationship is to help someone with joy and with no expectation of anything in return. It feels good, it trains your own sense of generosity, and it informs you of what the other person values. It also sets the stage for you to ask them something in the future. You don't have to offer to help in every circumstance, but make yourself available as a resource to people, particularly to people who are just starting out in their careers. I make myself approachable by posting my email and phone number online and responding quickly to legitimate information requests from people who are early in their careers if I feel I can help.

As you build your online network, don't neglect the people you already know. Your network is rooted in existing, real-life relationships, so put effort into connecting more regularly with the colleagues, clients, partners, and mentors who have firsthand experience working with you day-to-day and week-to-week.

Social media opens up incredible possibilities for strengthening your professional network. Make sure you approach online networking as an extension of how you interact with others in the real world: Connect with people personally by finding common ground, then build trust and long-term relationships rather than one-time transactions.

———————

Doug Camplejohn is vice president of product management at LinkedIn.

CHAPTER 22

How to Ask for an Email Introduction

by Ruchika Tulshyan

Email has made it easier to connect with anyone—and I've benefited professionally from introductions to new contacts around the globe that would've been unimaginable before the digital age. But requesting an email introduction through a current contact isn't without costs, especially for the person lending you their network, so I recommend asking thoughtfully and carefully.

One cost of your request is that it requires your contact to spend precious time crafting an email explaining

Adapted from content posted on hbr.org, December 23, 2019 (product #H05C2E).

why you and the other person should connect. One or two infrequent requests doesn't translate to much effort, but when you're getting multiple asks a week—like many busy people do—it can add up to hours of time spent introducing other people. This may be especially burdensome for women and people of color who, according to studies, are expected to do more favors and readily help behind the scenes.

Whether you're raising venture capital, looking for a new job, or seeking a friend in the city you just moved to, you can help lessen this burden—and make it more likely that your contact will agree to make the introduction—by including a forwardable email below your note to the person making the introduction. This shows empathy for the person you're making the request of and how busy they are.

A short blurb about yourself and your motivation for wanting to connect also forces you, as the requester, to think through *exactly* what you need from the connection. As a working mother who wears multiple professional titles, I'm less inclined to respond to a general introduction. I would much rather the person spell out what exactly they're hoping to achieve from the connection. And I'm more likely to respond to a request from someone looking to make a new friend rather than a vague request to "connect over mutual interests."

To write an effective forwardable email, consider the following.

Introduce Yourself Briefly

The point of the forwardable email is that it explains everything the person you're looking to be introduced to needs to know about who you are. Begin the email with a few lines—I recommend about three—detailing who you are and the information that's most pertinent to the request at hand. When I'm requesting an introduction to make a new business connection, I usually don't include that I'm an adjunct professor, for example. When crafting these, think "Twitter summary," not full-length professional bio.

State Your Motive

Next, be extremely specific about *why* you want to connect. Again, I recommend no more than three lines. "I'm looking to meet an investor for my food business," or "I've written an op-ed that I'd like you to consider for publication," or "I am looking for advice on how to apply to a leadership program at the university where you teach" are all clear motives. This brief paragraph should also include any other information salient to the request— details about your business or background that would be important for the other party to know in context of your request.

Do Your Homework

Show that you've researched the third party. If you're raising funding for your food business, spell out that you're hoping to meet Sarah because you know that she's an investor in the food industry. Or that Jane is the opinion editor at the local paper. Or that Jamilah handles student advising at the college you're applying to. Try to avoid generalities like, "I'm looking to meet people in the field." Also, double-check the spelling of their name. I've had a number of forwardable emails recently refer to me as "Ruckika," "Rachika," and "Rushika," and I'm less inclined to spend time responding to someone who can't take the time to get my name right.

Make It Easy for Them

Close the forwardable email with an easy way to connect with you and meeting times. I usually end with something like, "I'm based in Seattle and would be happy to meet you at your convenience on most weekdays for the next month." If you use an online calendaring software like Calendly, send them a link to your schedule. Also, close the email with a link to your LinkedIn profile and website so no one involved in the email—the person making the introduction or the person receiving the forwarded email—has to spend time researching you.

Expect a Double Opt-in Introduction

The forwardable email also allows the introducer to ensure the other party is open to the connection, so they can make a double opt-in introduction. I even include that in my forwardable emails by writing: "Please feel free to use the below forwardable email to check if Sarah is open to connecting with me." That way, the introducer has a seamless way to check in with their contact by writing: "Dear Sarah, please see the request from Ruchika below. Would it be OK to introduce you two?"

Send a Calendar Invite

Once your email has been forwarded and the other party has responded affirmatively to meeting, it's your responsibility to send a calendar invite with dial-in information and, ideally, a short agenda to outline why you're meeting. This can be the title of the meeting request or a more detailed agenda, if relevant. When sending the calendar invite, write your name first so that's what your contact sees on their calendar. For example, if I was to send a calendar invite, the meeting title would be "Ruchika/Candour to connect with Sally on op-ed." This is especially helpful when meetings are being set well in advance.

Most Important, Express Gratitude

I still get a number of requests that don't include a basic "thank you" or "please." Even after fruitful connections are made, I often find out about them on social media. When possible, circle back with the introducer and write a short note letting them know how the connection went. They are more likely to make another introduction if they know you appreciated it.

Close to 300 billion emails are sent and received each day, and that number is only expected to rise. Rather than contribute to the noise, make it easier for those helping you out. This means putting thought and care into introduction requests, which will help you make more meaningful connections and expand your network.

And, given the extra burden women shoulder to be helpful, here's hoping forwardable introductions can distribute some of those expectations more equitably.

———————

Ruchika Tulshyan is the author of *The Diversity Advantage: Fixing Gender Inequality in the Workplace* and the forthcoming book *Inclusion on Purpose: An Intersectional Approach to Creating a Culture of Belonging at Work.* She is the founder of Candour, an inclusion strategy firm.

Overcoming Distinct Networking Challenges

CHAPTER 23

The Secrets of Successful Female Networkers

One oft-cited reason why more female executives don't advance to top management jobs is their lack of access to informal organizational and industry networks. Some people blame unconscious bias: High-ranking men connect more easily with other men. Others cite professional and personal obligations, from office housekeeping to child-rearing, that disproportionately fall to women, leaving them less time to develop professional relationships.

But some female leaders do establish strong networks—and they win greater influence and more-senior positions as a result. What are they doing differently?

Adapted from an article in *Harvard Business Review*, November–December 2019 (reprint #F1906A).

A new study sheds light on their strategies. "I was talking with many women about how to improve their networks, the challenges they face, and what they and their organizations could do better, and I realized that all the studies on the issue were pretty old and narrow," explains Inga Carboni, a professor at William & Mary's Mason School of Business and the study's lead author. "I couldn't answer their questions."

The researchers analyzed data collected from 16,500 men and women in more than 30 organizations across a range of industries over the past 15 years. Then they interviewed hundreds of female executives. This led them to identify four characteristics that distinguish the networking behaviors of more-successful women from those of their peers. In some cases those matched the behaviors of high-performing men; in others there were subtle but important differences.

When shaping their professional networks, top women were:

Efficient

Studies, including the new one, show that women generally absorb more collaborative demands in the workplace than their male peers do. But the female managers with the strongest networks "recognize that every 'yes' means a 'no' to something else," says Babson College's Rob Cross, one of Carboni's coauthors. He notes that one Silicon Valley executive he knows has adopted that idea as her mantra. Although these successful female networkers might feel an identity-driven desire and a stereotype-influenced pressure to help colleagues out and be team players, they try to resist. They prune nonessential appointments from their calendars, deflect low-priority decisions and requests, run streamlined meetings, insist on efficient email norms, and set aside time for reflection and high-level thinking. At the same time, they make the most of their collaborative strengths and inclinations by working with others in a way that establishes or enhances key relationships and ups their visibility.

"At every level in organizations, women are more likely to be sought out for advice," Carboni says. "And when asked about the downsides of saying no, every woman I interviewed said they'd feel bad." But she emphasizes that the research is clear: The female executives who rise to the top are "more strategic and thoughtful" about how they spend their time. Organizations can do their part by tracking unseen collaborative work, ensuring that it's evenly spread among male and female employees, and pushing all leaders, but especially women, to unabashedly prioritize their most important tasks.

Nimble

The researchers' data shows that most women's relationships, particularly those with female peers, are stickier than men's, growing stronger, more mutual, and more interwoven over time. Carboni and Cross note that this can occasionally be a positive—for example, an old contact might offer a new opportunity or employment prospect. But if you work in a dynamic organization that requires rapid adjustments to changing demands (and who doesn't nowadays?), always relying on the same people can hurt your performance.

Successful female networks are more fluid. High-ranking women know when to deemphasize old connections in favor of new ones (whether by proactively cutting ties or by simply failing to maintain contact). For example, says Cross, "when you're at an inflection point at work or are embarking on a new project, you want to think about your goals and who will help you reach them—whether those goals are political (gaining early access to opinion leaders), developmental (supplementing skills gaps), innovation-oriented (searching for new insights), or related to best practices (finding people who know efficiencies)." He acknowledges that some women find this inauthentic, even Machiavellian, but notes that men interpret the same behavior as putting the work first. He says it's OK to have a "tenure bell curve" in professional relationships. Women should, of course, maintain some long-known advisers. But they should consistently initiate new connections, and organizations can help them by instituting processes such as network reviews at the start of new assignments or during performance evaluations.

Boundary Spanning

The highest-ranking, best-networked women connect with people in a wide variety of functions, geographies, and business units. Again, less successful female networkers tend to shy away from the tactic because it feels uncomfortable or overly promotional. "We heard from women that they liked their own communities," Carboni says, whereas spanning boundaries made them wary of "backlash" and "stressed out." But that behavior is critical to accessing new information, leading innovation, and

"YOU'RE CLOSER TO EVERYONE THAN YOU THINK"

Julie Lodge-Jarrett has worked at Ford Motor Company for 21 years, holding positions around the world. Currently the chief talent officer, she leads an initiative to encourage colleagues to develop better networks among the company's 73,000 salaried employees. She spoke with HBR about the special challenges female professionals face when trying to make connections. Edited excerpts follow.

As a female executive, how have you approached networking?

During my career, I've often been the only woman in the room. In developing a network, I always made sure it was authentic and purposeful. I didn't reach out to people because I thought they were important and I wanted them to know me. I tried to figure out whom I needed to know and why and set up meetings to pick their brains. When you approach it as a learner, people want to share their insights and experiences. Later, when I had more questions, I would ask those I'd forged a relationship with to connect me with others. In a company this vast, it may seem hard to create a broad network. But it's degrees of separation; you're closer to everyone than you think.

Are there aspects with which you've struggled?

I'm not good at saying no to collaborative requests. I always want to help. But one principle I've implemented for myself and across the organization is saying no so

(continued)

"YOU'RE CLOSER TO EVERYONE THAN YOU THINK"

that you can say yes to something more important: constant prioritization. Also, in the past when I made a connection, it was hard for me to let it go. But my mom always told me, "You can have a relationship for a reason, a season, or a lifetime." I'm starting to take that to heart.

What are you really good at?
Boundary spanning. A lot of that was just wanting to spend time with people who'd had different experiences, being curious, and feeling OK asking dumb questions. And I think I bring good energy to relationships. Most people who interact with me would probably describe me as positive or optimistic or can-do.

What research have you done on how your female peers at Ford have built networks?
We did some work studying women who rose to leadership positions but chose to opt out. One reason was that they weren't enjoying their work experience because they felt isolated and disconnected. The women leaders who stayed and continued to be successful had developed their networks early on and usually had

pursuing advancement, for both women and men. Cross suggests periodically considering the leaders in your organization and asking yourself, "Who isn't in my network but should be?" He advises approaching them "not with 'Here's what I need' but with 'Could we grab a coffee a mentor or champion who helped them build those networks in an authentic way.

What have you done to help women at Ford become better networkers?
We're trying group inclusion training, with men and women sharing their professional and personal experiences; we've found that to be much more effective than online bias-prevention training. We've begun to connect all our professional women's groups across skill teams and geographies; now the Women in Finance chapter can interact with the Women in India group, and so on. We're looking at a program that will help our high-potential women by training them in the action steps that drive successful network development. And we're increasing the dialogue between women and our senior leaders, the vast majority of whom are men. We have a "Mustang council" of key women who meet regularly to talk with Jim Hackett, our CEO. We want all our employees to expand their networks, not only internally but also beyond Ford, in the service of the company. We call it Raise Your Gaze.

and explore ways of working together?'" Companies including Ford and Booz Allen Hamilton have tried to institutionalize the practice by setting up cross-functional groups of female high potentials who meet regularly with C-suite executives.

Energy Balanced

More than two decades' worth of research shows, perhaps not surprisingly, that the highest performers are seen as the most energizing people in their networks—as the type of colleague who makes the work more engaging, which then drives better performance. But men and women are expected to bring different energy to relationships, and this is where effective female networkers set themselves apart from less successful women: They demonstrate both competence and warmth, both intelligence and emotional intelligence, as studies—the researchers' and others—suggest they must to build trust. "The most successful women don't downplay their knowledge, skills, and accomplishments; they show evidence that they can do things," Cross says. "But they also use humor, presence, and small gestures to signal caring and positivity, and they employ listening skills to spur creative thinking among their colleagues."

The researchers say they hope more women will adapt their networking behaviors in keeping with these four characteristics. They add that organizations have a big role to play too. "The goal is to embed these behaviors and practices so that they're the norm for everybody," Cross says.

ABOUT THE RESEARCH

Connected Commons report, "How Successful Women Manage Their Networks," by Inga Carboni, Rob Cross, Aaron Page, and Andrew Parker.

CHAPTER 24

Remote Networking as a Person of Color

by Laura Morgan Roberts and Anthony J. Mayo

In remote work situations, where people cannot rely on impromptu elevator conversations or watercooler chats with coworkers, the answer isn't to turn inward. In fact, the need for networking is even *more* important. Both external and internal networking can provide energizing social connections, firm and industry insight, personal affirmation, social support, and access to career opportunities. In particular, our interactions with people

Adapted from content posted on hbr.org, September 7, 2020 (product #H05U02).

whose backgrounds and perspectives differ from our own help us to become smarter, more creative, and better equipped to solve difficult problems.

Building relationships across difference does not come naturally or automatically. According to our research, networking can be especially challenging for professionals of color, who may not only experience general discomfort but also face unique challenges from not being perceived as powerful, credible, or resourceful—this deficit-based assessment often results in less outreach and relationship building. Professionals of color are also at higher risk of becoming isolated, struggling to navigate the racial boundaries at social events—in particular, they hesitate to share information about themselves, which limits their ability to be authentic at work and to build deep relationships.

The common mantra about working "twice as hard to get half as much" unfortunately rings true in economic data, which suggests that Black men and women must outwork and outperform their white counterparts to be seen as comparably skilled. Our research shows that this extends to activities like networking, where workers who differ from their counterparts report feeling excluded and marginalized, which makes it harder for them to believe that their social capital is valued.

However, remote work offers opportunities for professionals of color to network in ways that are more comfortable and authentic. By identifying these strategies, professionals of color can build new relationships that can elevate their careers over the short and long term.

Participate in Learning Communities

Virtual learning opportunities have proliferated over the past few years, providing opportunities to meet new people through workshops and discussion groups. Most colleges and universities are offering a variety of virtual seminars and other learning opportunities that support education and community building. Social media channels also offer interest-based groups where people can share resources and suggestions for dealing with work-related challenges.

Maintain Periodic Outreach to Champions and Sponsors

A common thread in the success stories of professionals of color is the support of a champion or sponsor—someone in the organization who not only provides advice but helps to create the conditions for new opportunities and increased visibility (see chapter 17 for more on sponsorship).

Network Through Community Service

Our survey showed that people are more enthusiastic about networking opportunities that are coupled with organized outreach events. Through these activities, they are more likely to meet people with common intellectual, business, or values-based interests. For professionals of color in our studies, these community service activities often include targeted outreach toward underserved and marginalized communities, such as mentoring youth of color and serving on not-for-profit boards. Community-based networking events are attractive because they tap into a sense of collective identity and higher purpose. They also help to counteract the belief that networking is purely motivated by self-interest.

Focus on Shared Networks and Organize Group Networking

We also discovered, through follow-up interviews and case studies of Black executives, that those most likely to invest in networking were able to reframe their perceptions of these activities from self-focused to other-focused. Conversations about networking became livelier when professionals talked about networks to which they *belonged* rather than networks that they *possessed*. A discussion of "my" network can be off-putting, casting one as an instrumentally focused power broker who may put personal advancement ahead of relationship strength. On the contrary, practices that build shared networks, that is, "our" [alumni/community group/professional association] networks, were evident in examples of people who were willing to make time in their busy schedule to field phone calls from strangers, answer informational questions from acquaintances, and help position other people for personal and professional success. As one professional of color stated, "Networking is essential to the soul. It is not about me."

Black alumni associations are useful exemplars of shared networks in that they meet regularly in regional groups and facilitate formal service and fundraising events, while also functioning as an insider channel for looping people typically in the margins into promising developmental opportunities. These unique forms of shared networks also provide rich contexts of cultural familiarity, which help workers and their families to create a sense of community in companies and cities where they may be demographically underrepresented. For instance, one Black executive said, "We can speak in shorthand to one another and say, How are you going to deal with this issue? We're all trying to accomplish similar things. . . . There's an inspirational level to it."

Participate in Remote Employee Resource Groups

The value of Employee Resource Groups has been called into question recently, under the rationale that they fail to promote inclusion. However, our findings suggest that ERGs provide an important vehicle for building and sustaining relationships—an especially challenging task for professionals of color—and that they should be systematically supported for the benefit of the workers and their companies. Now, more than ever, firms should invest in initiatives that support the strategic aims of ERGs to build community and strengthen business leadership.

Nonetheless, the burden of contact should not be borne solely by professionals of color. A lack of physical presence can exacerbate the "invisibility conundrum" that many professionals of color experience as being one of very few people like them in their organizations or fields—that is, their anomaly status often makes it more difficult to be part of key decisions and their "otherness" can make them invisible. The virtual environment can make matters worse, as it becomes far easier for connections to fracture, even inadvertently. That is why it is so important for professionals of color to ensure regular contact and interaction with their managers and their peers—and why managers and other industry leaders must proactively stay in contact with their colleagues of color as well.

Laura Morgan Roberts is a professor of practice at the University of Virginia's Darden School of Business and the coeditor of *Race, Work and Leadership: New Perspectives on the Black Experience* (Harvard Business Review Press, 2019). **Anthony J. Mayo** is the Thomas S. Murphy Senior Lecturer of Business Administration in the Organizational Behavior unit of Harvard Business School and the coeditor of *Race, Work and Leadership: New Perspectives on the Black Experience.*

CHAPTER 25

Making Time for Networking as a Working Parent

by David Burkus

Networks often seem to grow during after-hours activities, like after-work drinks, weekend off-sites, or faraway conferences. And that poses a problem for most working parents. How do you meet new people if traveling to conferences is out of the question? How do you strengthen connections with colleagues after work if you also need to hurry home for soccer practice? For many working parents, those problems don't get solved and their network growth ceases (and maybe even shrinks).

Adapted from content posted on hbr.org, May 23, 2018 (product #H04BMO).

But being a working parent doesn't mean the end of a thriving network; it just means you have to get a bit more creative and deliberate. I should know. As the father of two preschool-aged children and the husband to an emergency room physician, relying on organic network growth from after-hours events just wasn't feasible. I had to get intentional. I examined a variety of methods based on network research in my book *Friend of a Friend*. Here are a few evidence-based techniques I've found that work for me that may also help you.

Press Pause on Making New Contacts

When your kids are small, finding time to make new contacts can be a challenge, but there's a wealth of opportunity and new information that can come from old friends and former colleagues—in social networking jargon, your "weak" or "dormant" ties. And because you're already connected, reestablishing the relationship and catching up should be faster than making new connections. Weak ties are often more valuable than new contacts anyway, the research suggests. Don't overdo it, but find one dormant tie per week to reach back out to. Use their social media profiles to find updates on their life that you can use as a reason to connect, or take the 30 seconds to pass along a quick note when an article, video, or anything else brings that person up in your mind.

Explore the Fringes of Your Network

After you've reconnected with lots of dormant ties, start exploring who is on the edges of your network by asking for introductions from those weak ties. Like reaching out to old contacts, this a more time-efficient way to connect since there's an intermediary you both share. My favorite method was to ask multiple people "Who do you know in ____?" with the blank being the industry, company, geography, or whatever I wanted to get connected to. When the same name kept appearing on different people's list, that was a strong signal it was time to connect.

Get Virtual

When you do want to get to know someone, or reconnect with someone you know, think beyond the coffee or lunch date. With video technology, high-fidelity face-to-face conversation can happen without either of you leaving the office, or your home.

Practice Introductions

One of the most powerful things you can do to strengthen your network involves not meeting new people at all but instead connecting two contacts in your network to each other. You strengthen the network around you, provide value for both contacts, and become known as an overall generous person. And you can do it anytime of day via email (but make sure both parties know your introduction is coming).

Use Business Travel Wisely

There may be times when traveling for work is unavoidable, but you can make the most of your time away. If you're traveling to a conference, do some research ahead of time to find out who else is coming and schedule quick chats throughout the event—rather than hoping to meet some interesting people just milling around the coffee station. If you're traveling for a conference or event, see if you can arrive a few hours early or stay a little longer and use that extra time to reconnect with other contacts. My personal rule is that the number of overnights matter, but the number of hours in the day do not, so I try to arrive the earliest I can and leave as late as possible to sneak in a few more meetings.

Talk to Your Parent Friends About More Than Just Kid Stuff

Research on social networks suggests that your most valuable connections come from people with whom you share multiple contexts (called your multiplex ties). So examining non-kid interests, hobbies, and even work can lead to a stronger bond and more reasons to stay connected. Likewise, doing family events with your colleagues can be a valuable way to invest time in multiple areas of your life. One of my favorite moments from a recent family vacation in Washington, DC, was the time we spent walking the National Zoo with a work colleague and his family. We became closer friends and more valuable colleagues.

If a lot of these steps seem like a regular part of networking, that's because they are. . . . we just tend to forget about them. There's far more to growing a thriving network than attending networking events, working the room, and hoping you meet new people. Much of the work of networking involves taking care of the network you already have and slowly expanding it through current contacts. It's tempting to think that can only happen at after-work events or at big gatherings, but the truth is much of it can be done during hours you're already working.

You don't have to find more time to do networking; you just have to fit networking into the time you have.

————————

David Burkus is an organizational psychologist and best-selling author of four books, including *Leading from Anywhere*.

CHAPTER 26

How to Network Across Cultures

by Andy Molinsky

Picture this: You are at a networking event and see across the room a potential employer from a company you're interested in. You walk over to that person, look him in the eye, and say the following: "Hello, I noticed that you're from IBM. I'm very interested in IBM and would love to give you a sense of my background."

I posed this scenario to a group of professionals born outside of the United States and then asked whether they believed that, according to American cultural norms, the person's statement was:

Adapted from content posted on hbr.org, January 17, 2012 (product #H0086W).

(a) Too direct

(b) Not direct enough

(c) Appropriately direct

I also posed the same question to a group of American-born professionals, and the answers from the two groups were telling.

All the American-born professionals in the room answered (c)—that the statement was appropriately direct and was a reasonable way to begin a networking conversation in the United States.

The professionals born outside of the United States, on the other hand, saw the situation quite differently. A few with extensive experience living and working in the United States agreed with the Americans. However, the large majority didn't, answering (a)—that the behavior was too direct and assertive for an American-style networking event.

I then posed an additional question. Imagine that a few minutes later you see another person across the room from a company you're interested in. You walk over to that person and say the following in a tentative manner: "Hello, sir. My name is _____. I am so very honored to meet you. Would it be possible for me to introduce myself to you?"

Again, I had seminar participants assess the appropriateness of this statement according to American cultural norms: in particular, whether the statement was:

(a) Appropriately polite: When talking with someone at a networking event, especially someone
senior to you in either age or professional background, it is important in the United States to be
highly deferential.

(b) Too polite: Even when talking with someone
senior to you in age or professional background,
it is important not to be overly polite and deferential. It makes you look like you lack confidence
and professionalism.

Again, all American-born individuals answered
(b), whereas a large portion of the international professionals, many of whom were from India, answered
(a)—that the statement was appropriately polite for the
situation.

The ability to network—to develop contacts and personal connections with a variety of people—is a critical
skill for any global business leader. The only problem
is that global networking can be extremely difficult to
do when the rules for networking vary so dramatically
across cultures. In fact, these cultural challenges can be
so strong that many of the young foreign-born potential global leaders that I know often purposefully avoid
networking opportunities in the United States—despite
how important these opportunities can be for developing their careers.

So what can be done? In working with young global
leaders like Ravi over the past 10 years, I have found
three key tools for success in learning to adapt behavior

across cultures in a networking situation or in any other situation where you need to switch your cultural behavior to be effective in a new setting.

Learn from Those Around You

Watch carefully how others operate in networking situations, and learn what behaviors work and don't work in that setting. Customize your own approach from what you observe to develop a style that feels authentic to you and that is also effective in the new setting.

Master the New Cultural Logic

Learn the rationale for this new behavior from the perspective of the new culture. Learn, for example, why "small talk" is such an important part of networking in the United States. Understand from the American point of view why it's actually appropriate to speak positively about yourself and your qualifications. Master the logic of the new culture, and the behavior will feel much more comfortable to perform.

Finally, Practice!

Practice multiple times, ideally in settings that mimic the stress and pressure of real situations. Integrate the behavior so deeply into your psyche that it becomes your "new normal"—something you do naturally and instinctively.

Use these tools and you will master networking in no time. The bonus is that you will also learn a method that you can apply to any other global leadership situation you face—which perhaps is the greatest learning of all.

Andy Molinsky is a professor of organizational behavior and international management at Brandeis University and the author of *Global Dexterity* and *Reach*. His work helps people step outside their personal and cultural comfort zones.

CHAPTER 27

Networking Skills for Professionals from Underrepresented Backgrounds

by AiLun Ku and Ray Reyes

Professionals from historically underrepresented backgrounds (including BIPOC professionals, first-generation college graduates and white-collar workers, and those from low-income households) are often told by well-meaning advisers to "network for opportunities" without further guidance. But without understanding how to navigate the hidden rules of engagement—the "cheat codes" that are passed down generationally among predominantly represented groups—many of these professionals are unable to gain entry to the majority white and privileged networks that control access to quality jobs, projects, and resources. For underrepresented professionals, networking can feel like negotiating a labyrinth blindfolded. Many believe they need to present a fabricated and inauthentic version of themselves to have a better chance of getting past a heavily guarded gate into the land of career opportunities.

We believe that there is a better way for underrepresented professionals to network, a way that allows them to garner support and access and move their careers forward while remaining true to themselves. In our work as executives at The Opportunity Network, a nonprofit devoted to supporting students from underrepresented backgrounds through college and into thriving careers, we have seen thousands of individuals grow their professional networks and use them successfully to advance at work.

If you are a member of an underrepresented group, especially if you are early in your career, this is a paradoxical moment. Despite the rhetorical support that most workplaces now profess for greater diversity, equity, and inclusion, reality hasn't caught up; the benefits that professional networks grant still skew away from those faced with systemic barriers. But that doesn't mean you can't network successfully and amass social currency in the workplace. To build a wide and diverse professional community that will help you move up—and ultimately help you bring up others along with you—you must understand and navigate three lingering networking paradoxes that affect underrepresented individuals. Let's explore each in turn.

The Authentic-Self Paradox

The first paradox is the tension between code-switching and authenticity. Cornell professor Courtney McCluney and her coauthors describe code-switching as behavior in which one changes their "style of speech, appearance, behavior, and expression in ways that will optimize the comfort of others in exchange for fair treatment, quality service, and employment opportunities." Being falsely perceived as "unprofessional" due to unconscious bias or divergence from dominant norms has real consequences: It can limit access to opportunities, information, and resources and ultimately derail career advancement. In response, professionals from historically underrepresented groups, particularly BIPOC professionals, often choose to weave code-switching into their workday. They may adjust their self-presentation by mirroring the norms, behaviors, and attributes of peers from dominant groups. In the networking context, the drive to code-switch is heightened. Ongoing concern about meeting unknown—and possibly biased—people in situations that are layered with subtext and unspoken rules discourages underrepresented professionals from entering networking in spaces as their authentic selves.

However, code-switching is merely a tool for survival, not the answer. Beyond placing the undue burden of conformity and assimilation on people from historically underrepresented groups, code-switching calls for the erasure of one's identity, a sacrifice too harmful to sustain. Code-switching ensures safe and vacuous interaction, but it prevents you from making real connections and decays overall well-being in the long run. How can you extend yourself to others when it isn't safe to show up as yourself authentically? How can you be your best when you can't be you?

To manage this tension, we encourage you to reveal your authentic self gradually. The gradual-reveal approach doesn't ask you to contort your identity to fit another mold. Instead, it allows you to remain true to yourself while asserting your agency in which parts of yourself you want to share and when.

First, understand that how much to disclose at work is a balancing act for everyone. While your CEO probably feels safe showing up at work, they aren't going to share all the details from their Saturday night, and you shouldn't either. Your colleagues are not your friends and family, and total disclosure is not your goal. Set and maintain professional boundaries while observing the extent to which racially based comparisons, however subtle, drive social interactions in your workplace. Next, put out a feeler—share as much of your authentic self as you feel comfortable and safe doing with a single colleague or a small group. Pay attention to how your colleague responds, and match yourself to the intensity and depth of the exchange. If the exchange is reciprocated and mutually beneficial, you may feel safe to reveal more.

The gradual-reveal approach can be challenging to implement in networking settings where you'll be meeting people who are truly unknown to you. Whenever possible, lean on a trusted connection from your growing network to gather information in advance. If you do end up in a conversation in which a gradual reveal isn't going well, be prepared to politely move the conversation to a neutral topic and then bring it to an end; this person isn't likely to be a supporter, and you don't need to waste your time with them.

The Gatekeeper Paradox

The second paradox is that networks can be both stubborn gatekeepers and transformative door openers. The race to hire qualified, diverse talent is always on, and few organizations are keeping up. This narrow pipeline is chiefly the result of gated networks' tendency to value exclusivity and selectivity over diversity and expansiveness. This dated approach might have worked when firms were looking for cookie-cutter candidates from a short list of schools or a small circle of contacts, but these old ways simply do not achieve the new results that organizations are looking for.

The reductive "it's who you know" truism serves an outdated version of professional networks that are meant to keep the gates shut. These networks concentrate power among those who know about jobs, decide who else gets to know about jobs, who gets hired, who gets mentored, and who gets promoted. These most "in-the-know" networkers end up wielding outsized influence. Absent deliberate intervention, this power imbalance sustains homogeneous networks and perpetuates a homogeneous workforce.

However, the widespread awakening to the need for a more diverse workforce, technological advances, as well as "the Great Resignation" have flipped the script. With the wide adoption of social media, everyone has the tools to be a transformative door opener instead of a stubborn gatekeeper. Knowing this, we encourage underrepresented professionals to adopt an asset-based mindset: Recognize that you undeniably and intrinsically bring something valuable to the table. You have a reserve of tacit critical-thinking and problem-solving skills gained through your lived experience; you are fluently bilingual and can competently navigate between cultures with care and confidence because you do it daily. This self-awareness will enable you to network confidently and present yourself as the missing piece to employers' hiring puzzle. With an asset-based mindset you shift the "it's-who-you-know" approach from *getting past the gatekeeper* who knows about the job to *meeting the door opener* whose network is expansive enough to identify, attract, and recruit qualified talent (like you) from a candidate pool that has been historically untapped and underrepresented.

The Proximity Paradox

The final paradox requires professionals from underrepresented backgrounds to grow their close-knit professional circles into more expansive networks in order to increase their social proximity to networks of power and influence. Social proximity boosts social capital. And while it may seem like a contradiction, particularly if you are new in your career, social capital is intrinsically embedded in relationships in every direction, so we encourage you to invest time in building a network that is broad and deep and attend to it. Networks are living structures that require nurturing and pruning.

Of course, networking upward will help you gain access to mentors and sponsors, relationships that are critical to your long-term career success. But don't neglect networking laterally with peer and near-peer groups. Forming a network of peers boosts your self-confidence and provides the support you need to overcome the hurdle of soliciting new connections beyond familiar circles. Networking with midcareer professionals and near-peers also can help demystify the hidden rules of work that lie just ahead.

Finally, don't neglect reaching out to those coming up after you. A 360-degree network-building approach gives you connections and resources to meet varying needs. It also develops the habit of giving career support to others while creating the opportunity to receive it.

With an expansive network, you can build a personal board of directors, a group of trustworthy people ready to offer critical and encouraging feedback to you. This group could include a mentor, a personal friend, someone from whom you seek counsel, someone who is well informed in your workplace or industry, and someone who can connect you to opportunities. Among your board, you should feel safe and comfortable enough to honestly grapple with challenges, receive candid and constructive feedback, be supported with unconditional regard, and be able to show up as your authentic self.

Code-switching, barriers to entry, and navigating power dynamics all take their toll. Networking can be tiring to anyone—to underrepresented individuals, it can be downright exhausting. But the first step to overcoming these challenges is being aware of the three paradoxes and managing them proactively. This must be reinforced by personal wellness and self-care practices—and leaning on the support of your growing network—to remain balanced when obstacles inevitably arise.

We hope that you and every underrepresented professional has the chance to operate from a safe space with access to soft landings as you help close the opportunity gap by building networks and exchanging social capital. Expansive networks traverse ethnicity, language, geography, age, physical ability, gender identity (pay attention to people's pronouns), sexual orientation, social status, educational and training experience, and life experience. The more diverse you build your professional networks, the greater your access to information and connections and the sooner you will be in a place of abundant social capital and able to raise others up along with you.

AiLun Ku is President and CEO of The Opportunity Network. In addition, she is a management faculty member at the Institute of Nonprofit Practice. She is an alumna of New York University's Steinhardt School's Senior Leaders Fellowship and the Emerging Leaders Lab. She was also an MIT Media Lab Director's fellow in 2019. She received her MPA from NYU's Robert F. Wagner

Graduate School of Public Service and her BA from New York University's College of Arts and Science. **Ray Reyes** is Managing Director of Programs of The Opportunity Network, overseeing all organizational programs and program teams. Previously, he was an assistant director and career counselor at New York University's Steinhardt School of Culture, Education, and Human Development. He received his BA in English from Rowan University and his MA in higher education from the Steinhardt School.

Avoiding Networking Burnout

CHAPTER 28

How to Keep Networking from Draining You

by Jordana Valencia

Whether it's attending startup events, social gatherings, or happy hours, networking is a necessary part of every entrepreneur's life. But networking can be extremely draining. Imagine the countless hours entrepreneurs spend talking, traveling, and socializing with contacts and potential investors. Excessive social interaction can be physically and mentally exhausting for anyone. In fact, many of the founders I coach say networking

---

Adapted from content posted on hbr.org, May 9, 2018 (product #H04BFG).

sometimes robs them of the energy they need to work on actual business operations.

You can't avoid networking, but there are techniques you can use to prevent and cope with networking-induced exhaustion. Try the four tactics below. Not only do they provide short-term energy benefits but they also can help set you up for long-term success.

Determine Your Optimum Level of Social Interaction

Being with others can be enjoyable, but there will always be a point when it becomes too draining for you. Your mission is to figure out what that point is. To do this, list all your networking activities for the past four weeks and how many hours you spent per activity. Include in your list how much time you spent in activities where you had to actively meet and socialize with others, such as startup events or informal dinners. If you're a founder who spends significant energy prepping for social meet-ups by strategizing, researching, or rehearsing talking points, you can also include how much time you spent doing these networking prework activities.

Next, ask yourself: How many hours, in total, did you spend in networking activities each week? How did you feel at the end of each week? Which week drained you the most, and which week did you find energizing or at least realistically sustainable?

Tracking your networking hours and energy levels can help you be aware of your personal limits. I once had a client who was constantly exhausted from social events.

When we tracked his hours, we found he was spending 13 to 14 hours a week in networking activities—which was just too much for him! After some trial and error, we figured out that four to six hours a week was his optimum balance. You'll know you've hit your optimal level once you've found a social schedule that you can sustain in the long term and that leaves you feeling productive and energized at the end of the week rather than miserable and completely wiped out.

Choose Quality Over Quantity, Even If It Means Meeting Fewer People

Networking is often seen as a quantity game: The bigger your network is, the better off you are. But if you're already exhausted, trying to network with every interesting person who comes your way can backfire professionally.

Why? Because strong networks rely on great first impressions (see section 2). But positive first impressions require large amounts of mental energy, social strategy, and perspective taking, which you may not have if you're drained. Be strategic about which networking events to attend. If you can only network a few hours a week, choose a few high-quality, high-potential opportunities instead of spreading yourself too thin. Quality opportunities are those that provide long-term value, align closely with your immediate goals, or add variety and balance to your existing network of contacts. If your time is limited and you have an event that doesn't meet these standards, you're probably better off skipping it and conserving your energy for a different opportunity.

Bring a Coworker or Friend as Your Networking Partner

There will be times when you'll have to network more than you want. During these times, consider bringing a coworker with you to help you achieve your networking goals. If you're a solo founder, bring a friend who is knowledgeable about your business (you can even prepare them beforehand with a company and networking FAQ).

Bringing a partner with you serves three purposes. First, social support can help reduce exhaustion and burnout, especially if support comes in the form of a tangible service such as networking. Second, you and your partner can divide and conquer. This means that you can expend less energy and talk to fewer people but still gather a large number of contacts at the end of the night, thanks to your partner's efforts. To make this strategy even more effective, consider choosing a partner who is more extroverted than you or is naturally energized by social gatherings. That way they're intrinsically motivated and excited to socialize with others.

Use Microbreaks to Reenergize During Networking Events

Research shows that microbreaks, or nonwork periods of less than 10 minutes in duration, can help replenish a person's energy resources so that they're able to continue their work tasks. A one-minute break can be just as effective as taking a longer break of five or nine minutes!

To have a reenergizing microbreak, engage in an activity you enjoy that allows you to mentally detach from their networking tasks. A microbreak activity could be as simple as watching a funny video on YouTube or reading an engaging article on your phone. What's important is that you fully disengage from networking while you do the activity. To effectively disengage, try excusing yourself for a few minutes so that you can step away from the networking event. You can move to a less crowded area, such as somewhere outside the main venue, or to a private area where no one can disturb you, such as the restroom. The idea is to find a quiet space where you can engage in a fun activity and not be reminded of work. Even if they're just a few minutes long, effective microbreaks can give you the energy boost you need to get through draining networking situations.

———————

Jordana Valencia is the Regional Learning and Development Manager at Grab, Southeast Asia's leading mobile technology company. Previously, she was a consultant at Stanford GSB's Career Management Center. She has an MBA from Harvard Business School and a master's degree in clinical psychology from Columbia University.

CHAPTER 29

Five Ways to Say No to a Networking Request

by Dorie Clark

Successful professionals get them all the time: plaintive emails from long-ago colleagues, or college friends—or even those friends' adult children—seeking "an hour of your time" or a chance to "pick your brain" or an offer to "buy you a cup of coffee."

Early in your career, it can be flattering that someone respects your opinion and your network enough to want to meet you. But that quickly grows old. When

Adapted from content posted on hbr.org, September 19, 2016 (product #H034X7).

you start to receive more than a handful of requests per week—almost always for 30 to 60 minutes of private consultation—you would dramatically handicap your productivity if you tried to do them all.

Judging which requests to honor can be difficult, however. Of course you'd say yes if the person were a close friend. Similarly, it's easy to dismiss the requests if you don't know the person well or at all. But there's a large gray zone of casual contacts where you aren't excited to accept but would also feel bad declining. For those instances, here are five ways to say no, or at least a modified no, to a networking request.

Ask Them for More Information

Sometimes people will contact you because another person thought it would be a good idea—but they aren't really sure why. This leads to rambling, aimless conversations that you should do everything possible to avoid. Unless they can articulate why they want to meet with you—specifically—then it's best to say no. A good way to weed out the confused is to write back to their request by saying, "I'd love to see if I can be helpful. Can you tell me a bit more about what you'd like to discuss and how I can be useful to you, in particular?" Even this extra step will derail a significant portion of requesters, who won't write back at all. If they do, you can route them to the next step—referring them to other resources.

Share Resources

Once you have a handle on what information the other person is interested in, you can provide more-targeted help. Everyone will start out asking for a private call or meeting, but if you don't know them well, they need to earn that right—and they can do so by showing that they've already consumed all the publicly available resources. If you've created content on their topic of interest, such as blog posts, videos, books, or podcasts, you can send them a link to that material and say, "Your upcoming book sounds terrific. I've written quite a bit on the subject of how to launch your book successfully, and I think these articles will answer most of your questions. If you have further questions after checking them out, please feel free to write me back and I'm glad to help." If they do write back with a targeted, specific question, great—it shows that they're highly motivated and deserving of help. But the truth is, you'll lose another 80% of inquirers after this step.

Invite Them to a Group Gathering

If you'd genuinely like to meet the person but don't have time for a one-on-one coffee, you could invite them to a group gathering. This is incredibly efficient because you're connecting with multiple people at one time (I regularly organize dinner gatherings and virtual gatherings; see chapter 11), and they get the benefit of making additional new connections as well. If you're not interested in organizing an event, you can accomplish the same thing by inviting people to join you at events you're already planning to attend, such as a networking breakfast or industry mixer.

Defer Your Acceptance

Another way to protect your time is to defer the invitations you accept. For instance, I received more than 50 requests for podcast interviews this year, but I was busy writing my next book and launching an online course. My solution was to write back and agree to appear on the podcast but ask if we could delay it by several months; almost always, the host said yes. If you agree, you do have to honor your word and eventually do it. But corralling invitations into a time period when you have more flexibility can make the experience more enjoyable and beneficial for you.

Just Say No

Sometimes, a request isn't worth even a modified no. You simply have to decline. That may be because you have minimal connections to the person, or they've proven themselves to be somewhat clueless or entitled with their request, or perhaps you're simply too overwhelmed to say yes to anything. In that case, it's best to respond quickly but firmly. "Thanks so much for your kind invitation to meet up," you could say. "Unfortunately my schedule makes that impossible, so I'll need to decline. I'm wishing you the best with your project." They might be mad that you said no, but they won't be able to fault you for your promptness or your manners in getting back to them.

The internet era has made people far more accessible to one another—which is generally positive. But it's also emboldened our most tangential LinkedIn connections to reach out and ask for phone calls and in-person meetings that could take up all of your available time, if you let them. Staying productive and effective these days means knowing when—and how—to say a gracious no to the myriad requests that come our way so that we can focus on our own priorities.

———————

Dorie Clark is a marketing strategist and keynote speaker who teaches at Duke University's Fuqua School of Business and has been named one of the Top 50 business thinkers in the world by Thinkers50. Her latest book is *The Long Game: How to Be a Long-Term Thinker in a Short-Term World* (Harvard Business Review Press, 2021).

Sustaining Your Network over the Years

CHAPTER 30

How to Maintain Your Network over the Long Haul

by Rebecca Knight

Everyone knows it's important to build a network. But once you've made a connection with someone, how do you maintain it over the long haul so that you can call the person when you need help (for example, a job reference or a professional favor)? How frequently should you be in touch with your contacts? And how do you balance efforts to bring in new people while staying in touch with those you've known for a while?

Adapted from "How to Maintain Your Professional Network over the Years" on hbr.org, September 20, 2016 (product #H0352X).

Prioritize

First, "make a clear-eyed determination about who in your network you want to prioritize," says Dorie Clark, a marketing strategist and author of *Reinventing You*. She suggests "grouping your contacts into buckets" of categories—for example, current clients, potential clients, influential and powerful colleagues, and "friends who are real connectors"—and then figuring how best to allocate your attention. But priorities aren't always clear-cut, adds Francesca Gino, a professor at Harvard Business School and coauthor of "Learn to Love Networking" (chapter 2). There may be people you keep in touch with for no other reason than you enjoy their company or you have similar interests. "Think about the ways in which your relationships make [you] better off. If you're a happier person when you talk to a particular friend or colleague, make a point to do so on a regular basis," she says.

Show You Care

Next, Clark recommends thinking about the "different tools in your arsenal to stay in touch"—email, phone calls, coffee dates, social gatherings, and handwritten notes—and how you can best use these to nurture your relationships. The key to maintaining a professional network, she says, is to "be in the orbit" of the people you're trying to cultivate so that, if you require their assistance down the road, "you are still top of mind." The best way to do this is to "take steps that demonstrate you care about the other person and that you're interested in his or her life," she adds. "Be aware of when news or information triggers you to think of that person." Perhaps you read a book a former colleague might like, you attended a lecture about a subject she's interested in, or you recently met a connection of hers. "That's a good time to get in touch." Adds Gino, "Good relationships need to be nurtured. If you care for that person to be in your network, you should avoid contacting him or her only in a moment of need."

Be Strategic with Social Media

It's easy to stay connected to people from your past for digital eternity, but, cautions Gino, an overreliance on social media to maintain your professional network can be dangerous. "Just like a phone call is not the same as conversing in person, social media has a different level of fidelity," she says. "Sometimes social media tricks us into believing we have a strong connection with someone when, in fact, that connection only exists in that single plane of existence." Still, adds Clark, you can use social media to your advantage. You might, for instance, trade direct messages with your contacts on Twitter, repost content they've created on LinkedIn, or retweet blogs and articles they've highlighted. Even better, "take the conversation offline," she says. "If you notice that your friend was just promoted or had some other success, celebrate her win by giving her a call or sending her a note."

Offer to Help

Another way to remain in good standing with your contacts is to "look for ways you can be helpful to them," says Clark. "Listen carefully" to what they say and the challenges they face. "Perhaps your contact is struggling to help his son find an internship, and you know that your firm has them. Offer to make a connection. Perhaps your former colleague tells you she's interested in starting to do more video at her job, and you just read a book on the subject. Send it as a gift." Make sure your motives are pure, however. "Helping others is a fine thing to do, but doing so in order to gain favor only serves to demonstrate to those you intend to impress that you are shallow—the opposite of your goal," says Gino. "Being genuine and authentic and sincere is much more likely to create a sense of respect."

Don't Brag

Although it's good for your network to know about your professional successes and promotions, you don't want to gain a reputation as a braggart (see chapter 8). Gino recommends a milder form of self-promotion: simply "informing the other person about what you have been up to in a way that provides information he or she does not have." Clark concurs. "You don't need to bang the drum," she says. "If you have had a positive relationship with someone in the past and you're confident she thinks you are a good person, you don't need to go on a long-standing promotional campaign. Just stay in touch and express interest in her life. That'll keep a positive memory alive."

Don't Force Friendships

If there is someone from your past that "you want to keep up with and you've tried multiple times but the

WHAT SHOULD YOU DO IF YOU'RE GETTING GHOSTED?

by Kristi DePaul

When you're working to build a network, a sudden silence can shatter your confidence and leave you feeling confused and rejected. Rest assured, though, it's not just you who's getting ghosted. This phenomenon is manifesting on a broad scale and in a number of ways in the workplace.

Consider Your Approach

When it comes to building relationships, are you playing the long game? Or have you perhaps connected with someone and then, without missing a beat, sent along a personal request?

Pinging weak ties for favors makes your entire interaction seem transactional and frankly, more than a little exploitive. If you've been looking at online networking as a shortcut of some kind, know that strategy will likely backfire—leading to you getting cut off by new contacts.

Embrace the Awkward

If you're unable to let go of unresolved conflict (a tendency known as the Zeigarnik effect), you're not alone. Even if the person who ghosted you did so to avoid an awkward exchange, they are likely replaying it on some level as well.

(continued)

WHAT SHOULD YOU DO IF YOU'RE GETTING GHOSTED?

That might be the reason the ghosting is happening in the first place. For example, the person who initially violated the social contract (abruptly leaving an otherwise pleasant exchange in total silence) may feel there's no way to bring the conversation back on track. This is where your next move can be crucial.

Instead of letting their disappearance haunt you, send a brief, lighthearted message and leave the door open for them to reconnect or to simply let you know what's going on.

Give it a few business days. They might surprise you and share that they've been working on a major deadline or have been dealing with some issues that came up outside of their job.

If you don't hear back—yes, even if you can see that your message has been read—then move right along. Remember: An acquaintance doesn't owe you a response.

What if it's a recruiter who has suddenly gone silent? Perhaps the role they were pursuing you for was abruptly eliminated, or maybe they found a more suitable candidate. Either way, they should respond. If you've sent two follow-ups within a couple of weeks and they still haven't gotten back to you, it's time to write this opportunity off.

What If You're Guilty of Ghosting?

If you're reading this and even mildly cringing throughout, you might be a ghost. Know that your dangling conversations can, however, have a clean ending. When writing this piece, I knew I had to wrap up my own professional ghosting. So I sent the following email response that was about, oh . . . eight months late.

> Hi [Name]—I'm so sorry to have left our last conversation hanging. You have probably landed an amazing job by now or are busy with other projects!
>
> In any case, I wanted to apologize for dropping the ball on our communication, as I clearly did (the tough past year notwithstanding). And I'm also reaching out to see if you might still be interested in freelance work.

Perhaps appropriately, I never heard back. (Touché.) But my mind is at ease, and that was worth every second of wincing before I hit send.

Kristi DePaul is a writer, speaker, and global citizen who is passionate about technology and education as vehicles for upward social mobility and access to greater opportunities. She has written over 250 articles and blog posts on the remote work landscape, and her work has been cited in research reports from international think tanks and universities. She is founder and principal at Nuanced, a thought-leadership firm focused on the future of learning and the future of work, and serves as CEO of Founders Marketing, a fully remote content marketing company.

Adapted from "So, You Got Ghosted—at Work" on hbr.org, May 12, 2021.

other person just doesn't seem to have that same desire," it's probably a sign to give up, says Clark. "Maybe he's just really busy or his spam filter is particularly aggressive," but it's also likely he's not interested in staying connected. Gino agrees. "Don't become overly concerned with connections that aren't mutual because, just as with other relationships, seeming desperate only makes you less desirable," she says.

Regroup from Time to Time

Every six months or so, Clark recommends doing an audit of your professional ties. "You need to look at your list of contacts and ask, is it still accurate? Who should I add? Who is no longer quite as relevant?" Over time, Clark says, "you will cycle people" in and out of your network. This doesn't mean you won't talk to them, of course; it's just not going to be as often. Bringing new people into your circle and staying in touch with longtime contacts "shouldn't feel like a balancing act at all if you're doing it well," says Gino. "Continuously mix old and new when possible"—that is, introduce people you've just met to others in your network, which gives you an opportunity to learn more about both of them. "This opens up relationships that may have stagnated," she adds.

Case Study 1: Stay in Touch by Offering to Be Helpful and Expressing Interest in Your Contacts' Lives

Omar Qari owes a good deal of his career success to the power of networking—particularly one networking event.

Back in 2011, when he was an MBA student at Wharton, he attended a talk by one of the founders of Tech-

Stars. Before the talk began, he found himself in conversation with Talia, a "bright and energetic" undergraduate. "We both shared a passion for mobile payment technology, and we were geeking out on it together," he recalls.

Omar mentioned that he was looking for a summer internship with a startup, and Talia offered to introduce him to Charles, her former boss at Foursquare.

At Foursquare, Omar developed his own positive relationship with Charles, and he also met another developer, Ted Power, with whom he decided to found Abacus, an expense management service that helps companies reimburse employees.

When Omar returned to campus, he kept in touch with Talia. They emailed regularly and met for coffee from time to time. "We had both worked at Foursquare, and it was fun to swap war stories," he explains. "She also talked to me about how she was interested in moving into the investment space, and I offered to help her think through the type of company she might like to work for."

Omar also made it a priority to stay in close contact with Charles. "We emailed once a month, and we connected on the phone every other month," he says. "I would leverage his professional expertise and bounce ideas off him. At that point, he was interested in doing something in an early-stage startup, and he was experiencing it vicariously through me."

Charles eventually left Foursquare and moved on to Bessemer Venture Partners, an investment company. Not long after, Talia joined him. And, in 2014, just as Abacus was winding down its time at the Y Combinator accelerator, Bessemer became the first large-scale investor in the company.

It might be a stretch to say that a chance encounter with Talia is what got Abacus up and running, but Omar says it's not too off-base either. "I think of Talia as the ultimate loose tie," he explains. "We are not in constant touch now—she moved to the West Coast—but I know that if I called her, we'd pick right up where we left off. We are connected in so many different ways."

Case Study 2: Ask Questions and Don't Self-Promote

When Liz Graham moved to Boston she had an "aha!" moment about her life and career.

"I decided that I wanted to work at a company headquartered in the city, and I realized that I needed to expand my network," says Liz, who had worked for many years in the cable industry in New York and before that as a corporate attorney. "I needed to invest the time getting to know VC companies, local startups, and learning more about the players in the Boston scene."

So she did everything she was supposed to do. She reached out to college and business school friends living in the city, she attended networking events and industry-specific seminars, she accepted invitations to speak on panels, and she got in touch with local executives and invited them for coffee.

But her most fruitful networking took place on the tennis court. She was out hitting balls one day when the man on the court next to her—named T.S.—asked if she was interested in a match. "As it turned out, we were both in job-hunting mode—he had just left Zipcar—and so between sets, we talked about the kind of environment we wanted to be in, what we love doing, and what opportunities we were looking for."

Liz talked about her career but not in a self-promotional way. "It's a delicate balance," she says. "I tend to ask a lot of questions. I probe the other person. Naturally they will ask me questions, and that's when I talk about my story and experience."

Liz and T.S. traded email addresses. Soon, T.S. landed a job as the controller at Wayfair, the online furniture company, and Liz got a job at Hubspot. Over the next few years, the two stayed in touch. They would play tennis from time to time and exchange emails about their jobs and lives. T.S.'s child went to the same school that Liz's children had, and she often inquired about how the child was doing. She also reached out to him on social media. "When Wayfair had its earnings, I would send him a note of congratulations," she says.

When Liz saw that Wayfair's vice president of sales and service position was open, she was immediately interested and again reached out to T.S. He helped provide an introduction to the hiring manager, which jumpstarted the interview process, and Liz eventually got the job. She acknowledges that she has her tennis hobby to thank for it. "When you're doing something you love," she adds, "networking feels easy."

———————

Rebecca Knight is currently a senior correspondent at Insider covering careers and the workplace. Previously she was a freelance journalist and a lecturer at Wesleyan University. Her work has been published in the *New York Times*, *USA Today*, and the *Financial Times*.

CHAPTER 31

How to Reach Out After Losing Touch

by Jodi Glickman

What's worse than having the perfect person to reach out to about a job opportunity, a career switch, or an impending move to Asia, and not being able to do so because you've lost touch? How many people have you come across in your life who suddenly might help your cause, personally or professionally, but whom you haven't seen or spoken to in ages—and whom you perhaps feel guilty about popping up to contact only now that you need them?

The bad news is that it happens more often than you might think. The good news is that it's entirely possible

---

Adapted from content posted on hbr.org, December 9, 2010 (product #H006KQ).

to reconnect with people, even if it seems preposterous after months or years gone by. The passage of time is not a good enough reason to let a potential connection go to waste. If you have someone you've been meaning to reach out to or someone you're dying to reconnect with, here are three easy steps to make that potentially awkward exchange much less painful and potentially even fruitful:

1. Acknowledge the lapse in time.

2. Explain the "Why now?"

3. Offer a quid pro quo.

Acknowledge the Lapse in Time

There's arguably nothing more awkward (or annoying) than receiving a call or an email from someone you haven't heard from in ages who acts as if you're best buds or assumes you know (or care) about their current life. It's disingenuous and ineffective. On the other hand, glossing over a long-term lapse in communication is akin to ignoring the elephant in the room. You both know it's out there.

Instead, acknowledge the lapse of time up front and center—and give that time period some rationale or context. Have you been off at university completing your studies? Working or traveling abroad? Did you leave your profession to try something new? Did you have a family, get married, or change careers? Or have you just been completely busy and self-absorbed? Whatever the reason, you need to acknowledge it.

- Lance, I wanted to reach out to say hello. I know it's been ages since we've spoken, but I've thought of you often over the years and I've always wanted to reconnect.

- Patricia, how are you? I'm sure you're surprised to hear from me—the last time we spoke, I was headed off to graduate school. I wound up moving to Washington, DC, shortly thereafter, where I've been for the last five years.

- Sean, hello and I hope you're well! I'm so sorry I haven't been in touch sooner. You've been on my mind for months, and I've just been completely consumed by a crazy work schedule.

Explain the "Why Now?"

There are infinite reasons why you'd need or want to reach out to someone after losing touch. Presumably, you either have an agenda to pursue, you want to reconnect just for the sake of having them on your side if and when you do have an agenda, or you actually owe them something that you never followed up on.

In any of the above cases, it's important to think about why you're reaching out now, after all this time, and be transparent about your motive. The "why now?" should include both the transition or event that prompted you to get in touch and your agenda, if you have one. To wit:

- I wanted to reach out to you to let you know that I'm headed to Asia next month to work in GE's plastics division. Last I heard you were working in Tokyo. I thought you might be a great person to reach out to before heading abroad.

- After leaving the firm following the birth of my daughter, I recently came back online, and I'm thrilled to be working with the consumer retail sector again. I was hoping you'd have time to sit down for coffee and catch up; I'd love to hear your perspective on how the industry has changed.

- I've just begun the application process to graduate school, and I know you had a great experience at Duke. I was wondering if you might have some time to talk about your MBA experience with me.

Offer a Quid Pro Quo

Finally, throw in an offer of help or reciprocity for good measure. Be gracious and generous (*Thanks so much in advance for your help, I look forward to hearing from you*) and emphasize that you'd like to be helpful to them as well to the extent possible. You're much more likely to get a response when you think about a two-way benefit and not just how you can take advantage of the other person's expertise or connections.

As for me, I ran into a classmate in Ithaca, New York, one summer who was the entrepreneur in residence at the Johnson School. I told him excitedly about my business, and he generously told me to give him a call for some over-the-shoulder advice. Sadly, I let the ball drop. Life just moved quickly, as it often does, and when I finally got around to reaching out, it was nearly a year later. Nonetheless, I used my gumption and contacted him. I used the strategy above and then finished my "tail between the legs" email by letting him know that I'd certainly love to return the favor one day in exchange for his business expertise. It worked. Even though he had moved on from his role, Sean and I connected, and he was extremely generous with both his time and knowledge. We reestablished a relationship that should prove useful (and fun) to both of us for years to come.

Jodi Glickman is a keynote speaker and the CEO of the leadership development firm Great on the Job. She is the author of *Great on the Job*.

Index

Index

Notes

Notes

Notes

Notes

Notes

Notes

Notes

Notes

Smart advice and inspiration from a source you trust.

If you enjoyed this book and want more comprehensive guidance on essential professional skills, turn to the HBR Guides Boxed Set. Packed with the practical advice you need to succeed, this seven-volume collection provides smart answers to your most pressing work challenges, from writing more effective emails and delivering persuasive presentations to setting priorities and managing up and across.

Harvard Business Review Guides

Available in paperback or ebook format. Plus, find downloadable tools and templates to help you get started.

- Better Business Writing
- Building Your Business Case
- Buying a Small Business
- Coaching Employees
- Delivering Effective Feedback
- Finance Basics for Managers
- Getting the Mentoring You Need
- Getting the Right Work Done

- Leading Teams
- Making Every Meeting Matter
- Managing Stress at Work
- Managing Up and Across
- Negotiating
- Office Politics
- Persuasive Presentations
- Project Management

HBR.ORG/GUIDES

Buy for your team, clients, or event.
Visit hbr.org/bulksales for quantity discount rates.